A MECHANIC'S HANDBOOK TO THE GOD OF THE BIBLE

Why God Just Makes Sense

Michael O. Borthwick

A Mechanic's Handbook to the God of the Bible
Why God Just Makes Sense

by

Michael Borthwick

Copyright © 2022

ISBN: 978-1-7779128-0-2 (Print)
ISBN: 978-1-7779128-1-9 (Ebook)
ISBN: 978-1-7779128-2-6 (Audio)

Independently Published

First Edition

This book is dedicated to all those who are searching.

Isaiah 55:6

"Seek the Lord while He may be found; call on him while He is near."

Jeremiah 29:13

"You will seek me and find me when you seek me with all your heart."

ACKNOWLEDGEMENTS

Special thanks to:

- Alicia and Ignacio for giving me the inspiration to write out my testimony, which led to this book.

- Oliver, Andrew, Rebecca & Alex, definitely the best kids I could have asked for.

- Dan Lundblad for his never ending energy to help those in need.

- My wife, Kathy, for her ongoing support and encouragement.

- Jim Coyle for his enthusiastic support of the book.

- My mother-in-law, Marg Sussens, for helping with punctuation in the early stages.

- Tom St. Amand, who spent hours doing an initial edit. He called it his "Mornings with Mike" and taught me that if you can get the meaning across in one word rather than ten, one is the way to go.

- Cassandra Luther, who agreed to edit a book of 100 pages that turned out to be almost 300 pages, and who rose to the challenge and did an exceptional job.

- Affordable Christian Editing for their assistance in the final editing and layout of the book.

- The many others who read the book at various stages and gave very helpful input.

PERSONAL NOTE

How did I come to a place of sharing my life story on paper? It began when I wanted to help a couple where the husband was going through some serious health issues. His prognosis was not good, but feeling sorry for themselves wasn't an option. As a couple, they rose to the challenge to fight back with integrity and a spirit of hope. They had a very solid network of people praying for them and taking care of their physical needs. I felt God wanted me to be a part of that network, but I didn't want to only attend to some of their physical needs. I wanted to be part of helping with their spiritual needs. That's when God put it upon my heart to share with them my story of hope. So, I started to write out how God worked, and still works, in my life. I shared how God got a hold of my heart, and how this brought me peace and understanding in times of trouble. I am thankful that after they read my testimony, they wrote a nice letter saying it helped. I was very pleased that months later, the health issues were resolved, and all who were involved praised God for His goodness.

Hard times or trials seem to work in two ways: either they draw you closer to God, or they pull you away from God. I am so glad that this family was drawn closer to God through their ordeal. In my life, I have been both pulled away and drawn closer when going through tough times. Choosing to draw closer to God in times of trouble is always the better choice.

After giving a rough copy of my testimony to the couple whose husband was going through health issues, I started to refine it. After I was done, I had my friend Tom edit it. After re-reading my story, I felt God was leading me to share more about how my walk with Him progressed over the years after I accepted Christ. As the Bible doesn't edit out the failures of its saints, I didn't edit out my failures either. For I want all people, especially the broken ones, to be able to identify with some part of my story and to see that God's love is for everyone who will receive it. I also hope that I have shown from the Bible who God and Jesus Christ are, and in the process, answered some of the questions or concerns people have brought up to me over the years.

I am not trying to prove myself or what I believe to anyone. My goal in writing this book is to help those who are searching to find God—not a god, but *the* God...*the God of the Bible*. He is the only one that can give us true meaning in life. I couldn't find any worthwhile meaning in my life by pursuing happiness or peace in what the world had to offer. But I did find that peace and happiness in a relationship with Jesus Christ. I hope all who read this will place their faith in Christ and live out **Colossians 3:1–4:** *"Since, then, you have been raised with Christ, set your hearts on things above, where Christ is, seated at the right hand of God. Set your minds on things above, not on earthly things. For you died, and your life is now hidden with Christ in God. When Christ, who is your life, appears, then you also will appear with Him in glory."*

It is my prayer that as you read this book, light will be shed on the subject of why God wants a personal relationship with you through the Lord Jesus Christ. *"But God demonstrates His own love for us in this: While we were still sinners, Christ died for us"* **(Romans 5:8).**

May God bless His Word.

CONTENTS

INTRODUCTION

This book is about how a sincere prayer from my heart at twelve years old set in motion a series of significant events that brought me into a relationship with *the God of the Bible* in my early twenties.

My journey has taken a few twists and turns over the years, some by His hand and some by my own foolishness. But my story demonstrates how God's influence in my life set me free from the baggage that I had been carrying around, bringing me peace and contentment.

Hopefully, through sharing personal stories, some anecdotes, and God's Word found in Scripture, I will present a candid view of who *the God of the Bible* is and how my walk with Him progressed.

When I have spoken to people about God over the years, I have observed that there are many different views about who God is and how He interacts with us. For anyone who has questions or misconceptions about God, it is my hope that this book will provide some logical answers.

The most important element of these writings for me is giving the reader a comprehensive description of who God is, why we need Him in our lives, and how to enter into a relationship with Him as I did.

My Background

I was born in Sarnia, Ontario, in the spring of 1958, and it is where I have lived my entire life with the exception of three eight-week semesters at Fanshawe College in London, Ontario, where I studied for part of my Automotive Technician Apprenticeship Program.

After I finished my Apprenticeship in 1981, I wrote my Ontario Certificate of Qualification exam, acquiring my Ontario Mechanic's License.

I have been tearing apart mechanical things my whole life, and as I was growing up, my hands were always covered in grease and oil. My mom would get so upset with me because, no matter how many times she told me not to get my clothes dirty, I always came home covered in grease stains. I loved disassembling something to see how it worked and then fixing it…so much so that my curiosity led to my life's work as an auto mechanic; I like the fact that mechanical devices make sense to me by their structure and design.

When repairing a car and dealing with all of its different working components, the person doing the work has to properly follow certain rules. Those who think they can sidestep procedures when doing repairs, usually end up with a car in worse condition than when they started. If we have a firm understanding of how all of the systems work together on the car, and if we follow the rules and procedures from the manufacturer, we are able to repair just about anything.

This is why I love following God. When I came to understand how God works in our lives, and when that understanding grew through reading the Bible and prayer, I discovered that it became like mechanics to me: it just made sense. God's Word is systematically laid out in the Bible, just as mechanical thought is systematically laid out in design. As a mechanic, I have been trained to think systematically, and this approach works really well when studying the Word of God—to connect the dots from Genesis to Revelation.

The fact that His laws and rules don't change, and His ordinances are established from everlasting to everlasting, gives depth to my beliefs and convictions.

There will always be those who think they can step outside of God's rules, just like those who try to repair cars outside of following known procedures. And in the end, the outcome will always be the same: they will be in a worse situation than when they started.

I hope that whoever reads this will have, when he or she is finished, a better understanding of why I believe as I do. I pray anyone searching to find peace with God will find answers in this book.

I wrote this book on the assumption that, for the most part, people believe in God; however, if you don't believe in God, I hope that you will glean some truth from the following pages that sparks an interest to learn more about *the God of the Bible*. If you say, "Don't worry about me, Mike, I am okay," just let me leave you with these thoughts to ponder: **If I am wrong about God,** I still feel that I had a better life in the sense that God was in it, rather than not. **If I am right about God,** what implication does that have for you? I urge you to take the time to read on and find out.

1

HOPE

"Men can live about forty days without food, about three days without water, about eight minutes without air, but only for one second without hope."[i]

—Hal Lindsey

Without Hope, Life Loses Its Significance

Two men were in a POW camp. One of the men had the hope of seeing his family again, which helped him to endure the mentally and physically harsh conditions of life in prison; the other man's family had been killed in the war that was ravaging their homeland. To this man, there was nothing to live for; he had lost all hope. Giving up, he wasted away until he succumbed to death a few years after his arrival. In comparison, the man who had family waiting for him focused on the hope of seeing them again. He stayed strong and endured the very harsh conditions, year after year, until he was finally released as a free man.

Hope has the ability to encourage us beyond what our circumstances dictate. Hope always believes there is a light at the end of the tunnel. Of the two POWs, the man without hope became disoriented in the darkness of despair, which ultimately led to his death; but the other man, the one focused on being reunited with his family, pulled through. Just as I once did, many today have a poor understanding of the importance of hope to give significance and value to our lives.

How Hope Was Introduced Into My Life

In my early twenties, all that I saw was all that I knew. It seems I was always destined to be a mechanic, and I had no problem with this, for I liked working on mechanical things. My life seemed to be all planned out: complete my apprenticeship, obtain my mechanic's license, work on cars for the rest of my life, and at some point, move out of my parents' house and find a girlfriend. I would be living the dream.

Hope is a feeling of expectation and desire for a particular thing to happen. I didn't have to hope for anything, for everything I thought was going to happen was happening. That changed after a car accident in the summer of 1978 and a few more brushes with death in the years to follow.

During the late 1970s, information wasn't coming at us twenty-four hours a day; if you didn't watch the six o'clock news, you didn't know what was going on in the world. I didn't watch the news, and this narrowed my view on world affairs; it was as if I had a veil over my eyes, and that made me very self-centered.

I don't know if it was the tunnel vision or being self-centered that made me feel that my life didn't have much context, but what I did find out in the years to come was that when your world becomes all about you, it becomes really small, and the smaller it gets, the more insignificant it becomes.

The Pre-Accident

In the spring of 1978, I purchased a white, two-door, Canadian 1968 Volvo Amazon 122. It was my first car; it had very little power, but the stick shift made it fun to drive. The car was known to be a good rally car, and this was established by a Swedish rally driver named Tom Trana winning the European Rally Championship in Monte Carlo in 1963. The legacy of this car prompted me to try my unofficial luck at rally driving on the back roads of the Bruce Peninsula while on a camping trip. My rallying days were short lived, however, when my friend Mark and I were going around a corner a little too fast. The car rolled over onto its right side, sliding on the loose gravel and coming to an abrupt stop when the roof on the left side of the car, just above my head, hit a tree. Luckily, within a few moments, a pickup truck pulled up with a couple of guys who helped Mark and me roll it back onto its wheels. Once the car was upright, we were once again on our way, but definitely going slower than before.

You could say that I was a little bit of an aggressive driver; my rule of thumb was that if your foot wasn't on the brake pedal, then you should be pressing the gas pedal hard against the floor. This driving style didn't work out too well for me later that summer; it caused a near fatal accident, and that accident opened my eyes to the realization that my life didn't hold much significance to me.

The Accident

Mark, Olaf, and I were friends that grew up in the same neighbourhood, went to the same public school, and could always be found hanging out together. I was twenty years old when our little group of three was reduced to two when Mark headed out west for a job in the early summer of 1978. By mid-summer, Olaf and I were heading up to Algonquin Park in northern Ontario to camp for a few days. We headed out on a beautiful summer's day, and as we drove along with the sound of wind rushing through the open windows, we felt that all was good. Cruising on a two-lane highway just south of Bracebridge, we decided to stop for a washroom break on the side of the road. This is where my aggressive driving style got us into trouble.

Since I didn't want to hold up the traffic behind us, I pulled off the road without slowing down. I had done this many times before without mishap, but this particular time, it didn't go so well. The Bracebridge County road crews had just finished redoing the shoulders of the road, and I missed a warning sign about the soft shoulders. At the speed I was travelling, as soon as the front right wheel hit the soft gravel, the car was immediately pulled down into the deep ditch until we hit an embankment made up of large boulders that bordered a driveway and were propelled into the air. Amazingly enough, the car came to rest on the driveway, upright, facing the road, and still running.

As the car had spun through the air though, I had been ejected out of the driver's window onto the rocks below. Olaf stayed in the car and sustained a few bruises. I, on the other hand, hit my head and broke my right collarbone and was taken away by ambulance to the hospital.

That little Volvo was almost indestructible, but that was its last voyage. I am not the kind of guy who looks back and makes more out of something than it was, but when you are thrown out of a car window while it's flying through the air, the probabilities of getting seriously hurt or dying are quite high.

You would think that after cheating death and serious injury, Olaf and I would be glad to still be alive. But the very opposite occurred. After we got back home, Olaf and I talked about our adventure—actually, it was mostly Olaf giving me crap for wrecking his vacation. I told him my opinion of the outcome was, that at some level, it really sucked that I had survived.

How could a young guy in good health, who lived in a free country, with a good job and family, be disappointed that he survived a car accident? Because without hope, life loses its significance. The only hope I had was in what I could see, and what I was seeing at twenty years old obviously wasn't enough for me to put much value on my life. I saw life only as a means to an end, and that end was being buried six feet underground. I didn't know it at that time, but life is a precious gift from God. I also wasn't aware that when you are lowered into the ground, eternity begins in either Heaven or Hell. When I came to understand that my significance in life came from God, everything changed.

Thinking death is an escape from an insignificant life is the personification of hopelessness. For death without God wasn't going to bring peace to my soul; in fact, it's just the opposite.

I can truly say that I am glad my life didn't end on that summer's day back in 1978 because a few years after the accident, I found God. He gave my life the significance I had been seeking. He also gave me the peace that my heart desired and the direction that I needed. It wasn't always a smooth road—there were a few mountains to climb and some dark valleys to endure—but never again did I feel that my life wasn't significant. The reasons I felt like I did before the accident never returned once I came to know God personally. For I had hope that no matter what life threw at me, I wouldn't have to go through any of it alone. God's promise was to be with me every step of the way, and God is incapable of breaking any of His promises. The hope that I have placed in God has been tested a few times over the years, but it has never failed me.

The following pages contain my testimony of how God opened my eyes to the fact that I needed Him more than He needed me.

2

MY TESTIMONY

This is a story of how God brought me into His family through a simple prayer from the heart. My journey of enlightenment began in the spring of 1970 when I experienced a very traumatic event at the age of twelve. After sleeping out with a few friends in an old doghouse that had been transformed into a young boys' fort, I entered our family home early the next morning to find my older brother, Larry, sitting in our living room. This was odd because he was supposed to be away camping for the weekend. When I asked him what he was doing home, Larry didn't answer, but the look on his face was one I had never seen before.

My mom was at the door in the front room speaking in a hushed voice with a very distinguished man. She then came into the living room, motioned for me to sit on the couch with her, and sat down facing me. Tenderly, in a very soft tone, she told me that Steve, my older brother by six years with whom I shared a bedroom, had been killed in a car accident around midnight.

Steve had been with his friends, riding in the passenger seat, when a drunk driver went through an intersection and slammed into their car. Seat belts weren't worn in those days, and Steve had flown out of the car, hit his head on a traffic light pole, and died instantly. He had just turned eighteen and planned to start an apprenticeship to become an automotive mechanic when he graduated from high school in just a few weeks.

I had never felt emotional pain like that in my life. I can't remember much about what happened after I was given the news; I guess I went into shock. How does a person prepare anyone for news like that—a sibling gone, a child lost, never again to darken another doorway in our family home. God was not part of our family at that time, so the idea of Heaven was no comfort to us. To our family, *Heaven* was just a word brought up in conversation when someone had died and had gone to "a better place," not a concrete reality. It was simply a feel good, abstract idea—an idea that would be nice if it were true.

Later that morning, I remember being in the back room of our house where we kept our coats and shoes. Sitting on the floor with my back against the big stand-up freezer, I was alone, just staring out the back door. The sun was pouring in through the window, covering me with its warmth. I can't remember exactly what I was thinking about, but the warmth of the sun was making me feel a little bit better. In retrospect, I believe God was trying to intervene, to bring some type of hope into my situation. I wanted so much to understand this calamity that had been thrust into our lives, but for the time being, I just sat there and stared blankly out the back door. The explanation of this time in my life would come years later, but one thing was certain: nothing would ever be the same.

Sometime later, after the funeral service was over and my brother Steve was in his final resting place at the cemetery, life started to get back to normal—or at least to our new normal. Our tears had dried, but a deep sadness hung over our house for a long time. One night in my bedroom—which I now shared with Bob, my younger brother of six years—I was climbing into the top bunk for the night when I noticed a bookmark pinned to the wall. I don't remember what the writing said, and I don't even know how it got there, but I stared at the little cross on it, then folded my hands together, and for the first time in my short life, prayed from my heart to God, or to something, for some type of answers. As I mentioned, we were not a religious family; I don't think we even had a Bible in the house, and I couldn't tell you at that time if we had ever gone to church. Nevertheless, I prayed. I didn't know it then, but this was the start of my journey toward something bigger than myself.

When we ask questions, say to a higher power, I think it would be prudent to try to understand the seriousness of asking such questions. When the questions are answered, if we choose to disregard the very source and trivialize the answers, what consequences will there be? I think if we are going to ask the questions to a higher power, we must be ready to receive and then act upon the answers.

Here is my story of asking questions, of receiving answers, and of making decisions. It is a story of how not making a decision could have had a detrimental outcome and how pride could keep one in a holding pattern for years or, even worse, prevent one from finding true answers.

Six years later, I still had a feeling deep inside that something unexplainable was calling me. All that I had experienced up to that point in my life had left me unfulfilled and pondering the age-old questions of life.

At age eighteen, the prayer I had prayed six years earlier in my bedroom before a small cross went from wanting "some type of answers" to finding a more absolute *why*:

- Why was I here?
- What was my purpose in life?
- What's the plan?
- Why was there so much pain and suffering?
- Was there a Master of destiny?

Also, one of the biggest questions I had as I headed into manhood was where do I fit in? In the great scheme of things, where did Michael O. Borthwick fit in?

These were not the abstract thoughts of an adolescent teenager, but the reflective thoughts of a young man starting to leave childish things behind and hoping to make his mark in the world. The wild times didn't seem to hold the same appeal they once had; smoking pot now made me tired and irritable, while drinking made me act stupid.

An unmistakable feeling kept welling up inside me that there was something more to life. This unmistakable feeling kept hounding me to search for something more. I wasn't really sure what the "more" was, but that nagging feeling deep inside made me feel more than ever that if I searched for it, I could find it.

The Journey Continues

My progression to obtaining the answers to "why" continued one summer night. The lyrics of the songs playing on the stereo mentioned the very things in life to which I seemingly had no answers. The music, combined with the setting sun, stirred deep thoughts in me. Dusk brought shadows in my room, and the sun outside my window became the most beautiful shade of orange glowing across the sky. In a melancholic state, I stared out the window at the darkening sky as the brilliance of the setting sun streamed into my room, and the stage was set for my heart to start questioning my own mortality.

Just then, a light, warm breeze wafted through the window and I pondered what was going to happen when death came knocking. As I thought about that, the warm air drifting in through the window seemed to turn cold and, with the sun setting over the western sky, the room lost its feeling of comfort and warmth. I continued to contemplate the question of my mortality. An uneasy feeling came up from my soul, almost as if I felt a sense of urgency to deal with the question of death sooner rather than later. At the same time, I sensed that I was being pushed to continue considering the uncertainties of life, and the room grew even darker. Sitting in the dark, I quickly became weary of the questions swimming around in my head; I was in a spiritual battle and didn't even know it.

I turned my gaze back to the forming stars and the last rays of a beautiful sunset. I thought about the beauty that I had just witnessed as optimism grew in my soul. I remember thinking that an artist had to create such beautiful scenes and such wonders of nature, and if this fact were true, there had to be an author for life itself. There in the darkness with the stars shining, I asked my questions once more from my heart—for questions from the heart are always heard. I didn't realize it then, but I had made the most important decision of my life: I had unknowingly made the decision to find God.

My many questions started a sequence of events that would ultimately bring the answers to me. I had an intuitive realisation that with the answers there would come an expectation and a decision: I would have to decide for myself whether to accept or reject the answers I sought. In hindsight, I realize now that if the answers had come that night or the night of my first prayer, I would not have been able to accept them. I was not yet ready or prepared to respond with acceptance at that time.

Years passed during which I hardly ever thought of those perplexing questions. I was caught in a lull, and I knew it. It was one of those times in life where nothing, it seemed, was ever going to change. And to be honest, I didn't particularly want my life to change, for my life was good. I was in my mid-twenties, and I had quit drinking and smoking pot. I was also racing dirt bikes, which took up the majority of my time, and I had a good job and a girlfriend. My head was never so clear, and my life seemingly had some purpose. It was, I knew, a worldly purpose, but it was a purpose just the same.

The reality though, was ever since I had prayed as a twelve-year old boy to a cross on my bedroom wall, the preparations in my heart had never ceased. Even though I wasn't really looking for answers at that time, the answers to those perplexing questions were starting to be revealed, whether I liked it or not.

For some reason, I steadfastly resisted hearing the answers to the questions I had asked so many years before. I think it was because I had a feeling that my acceptance of the answers would bring about change, and there was comfort in familiarity; at this point in my life, I really wasn't looking for a change.

Regardless of how well or how badly things are going, or how out of control life can get, change is always a scary business. But the progression in my life over the years brought me to the point where I could not only somewhat comprehend the answers but could also act upon them. My own fears of the unknown were causing me to resist, but at the same time, these same fears were causing me to continue.

I wasn't aware of it at the time, but powers greater than I was able to comprehend were working to bring me to the place where I could understand and act upon the answers that were starting to be revealed. At the same time, opposite powers were trying to stop the process and keep me from dealing with my own mortality. Were these the powers of good and evil, with the good guiding me to enlightenment of truth and the evil keeping me in darkness, oblivious to the truth?

Looking back now, I understand that the answers to these questions and the choice to act upon them were the most important decisions I was ever going to make. It was also becoming quite clear that these decisions were more faith-based and involved something far beyond me. They were, in fact, far greater than something I could literally see, touch, and understand in my humanity.

I can't see gravity, for example, but I can understand it and see its effects. I was starting to learn that I couldn't see spirituality, but I was becoming strongly aware of its existence.

Now, in my twenties and for the first time in my life pondering spirituality, I came to define spirituality as the quality of being concerned with the human spirit or soul, as opposed to material or physical things. The tide was turning in my life; spirituality was becoming more important than it ever had been before. I knew something spiritual was happening, and I was starting to see the dots connect through my girlfriend, who I was living with at the time. She came home one night and announced that she was "born again." My response was, in essence, "What are you talking about?" She then started to talk about Jesus all the time, something that I found very annoying.

As time went by and she embraced her new life, I noticed a few personality changes that stood out: she became softer, less critical, and more affectionate in a very wholesome way. It was evident that she was taking this church stuff very seriously, and it was making a difference. While I saw it as church stuff, she always corrected me and said that it was a relationship with Jesus Christ—as though I knew the difference.

I thought it was all fine as long as I didn't have to give up my lifestyle and could basically remain the selfish man-boy that I was. Everything began changing, though, when she started telling me that I was a sinner who was going to spend eternity in Hell. I countered with the assertion that I was a good person who had nothing to worry about. This answer didn't satisfy her in the least and, to be completely honest, deep down, my words didn't really satisfy me either. It's amazing, really, trying to justify to God my entrance into Heaven by being a good person or just better than the worst of society.

Christ Was Clearly the Crux in All of This

I wondered what was going on in my head. I had asked for answers from a higher power, and it seemed that these answers were starting to unfold through my girlfriend's **personal relationship with Jesus Christ;** yet I was resisting the answers. Why? I can only go back to what I said before: it seemed like opposing powers were trying to stop me from dealing with my own mortality.

In a nutshell, she was saying that I was separated from God because of my sin and quoted from **Romans 3:20,** *"Therefore no one will be declared righteous in his sight by observing the law; rather, through the law we become conscious of sin."*

She also said that Christ was the only payment for sin and quoted **Galatians 2:21:**

> *"I do not set aside the grace of God, for if righteousness could be gained through the law, Christ died for nothing."*

My Good Person Theory Was Flawed

What my girlfriend was saying from the verses she quoted was that putting my faith in the Ten Commandments/The Law wasn't going to help me become righteous or justified in the sight of God. And since there was no justification for the sin in my life, I was guilty and condemned.

Then she clearly pointed out the seriousness of the situation: Hell. *"If anyone's name was not found written in the book of life, he was thrown into the lake of fire [Hell]"* (**Revelation 20:15**). In her estimation, Hell was where I was going to end up.

Well, she still hadn't convinced me, but the changes in her life were speaking volumes. She had a peace about her now; she was more caring and understanding, and we got along so much better. These changes in her personal life were softening me to her ideas about God, Heaven, and Hell. She was quick to point out that these ideas were not her ideas. Rather, she explained, they were the truths of what the Bible says will come to pass. After that, she pretty well left me alone, but before doing so, she gave me a book on Bible prophecy entitled *The Late Great Planet Earth* by Hal Lindsey. Through reading that book, I found some interesting answers to two of the crucial questions I had asked years before: Is there a master of destiny? And why was there so much pain and suffering in the world?

Now the dots were being connected very quickly, but I still wasn't ready to acknowledge that I needed a relationship with God like that of my born-again girlfriend. I was also hesitant to forge such a relationship because I wondered what my life would look like if I did become born again.

With this new standard of right and wrong my girlfriend was presenting, I realized that I was no saint. I began seeing my anger, selfishness, and swearing, to list a few things, in a different way—I was seeing them as wrong. And if they were wrong, I knew that coming to God would mean that I would have to change. But how much change would I be required to make? For example, would I have to start going to church on Sundays? Would premarital sex be out the window? Would my racing days on Sunday be over? I had a lot to consider for I wasn't so naive as to think that I wouldn't have to learn to put all of God's precepts into practice in my life if I made the choice to follow Him.

My Enlightenment

I came face to face with the reality of my spirituality and my physical limitation in just one split second of time. This was an unexpected enlightenment that was to thrust me into getting off the fence and making a decision of amazing significance. But the total magnitude of that decision would take years to transpire and is still transpiring to this day.

The questions I had asked from the heart many years before— as a little boy praying to a cross on his bedroom wall and then as an older teenager with more questions on a warm summer night in my upstairs bedroom—were being answered with clarity. These answers, one after another, were all pointing to God. This God was not the one I had always imagined: the old guy in Heaven in a rocking chair, stroking his white beard and pondering all that had gone wrong in the world. No, He was an all-powerful, all-knowing God who held the whole universe together in His hand. This was the God seeking me out because I asked Him to.

My final enlightenment came from an unexpected source. I was in an accident while dirt biking up the side of a hill beside a busy two-lane highway. Just before I reached the top, my front wheel hit a rut, causing me to be half knocked off my bike. This sudden movement caused my dirt bike to switch directions and thrust me down the hill. Ironically, the more I tried to pull myself back onto the bike, the more I pulled on the throttle, and the faster I went. Now, totally out of control, I was racing down the hill into a ditch, thinking that the deep ditch would stop me. It didn't. In fact, the ditch acted like a ramp propelling me into the air.

Somehow, I was still on my dirt bike, about six feet off the ground and sailing onto a busy highway outside of Brantford, Ontario. I remember thinking it was a no-win situation, either for me or for the cars speeding by. Everything in my brain went into slow motion. Still on my dirt bike in the air, I narrowly missed the back of a small car in the closest lane. Heading across the road towards a red Camaro in the far lane, I pushed myself off the bike and started to flap my arms to slow myself down. That did not work.

When the driver of the red Camaro saw what was happening, he tried desperately to accelerate out of the way. But still, the rear tire of my dirt bike hit the back quarter panel of his car. I will never forget the look on the face of the guy in the Camaro's backseat; he was ashen, and he had a look of utter disbelief—like he couldn't believe that he might get taken out by a flying dirt bike. I came down hard onto the pavement on my hands and knees; my protective riding gear saved me from getting hurt, but also made it easier for me to slide across the pavement into the path of a big Chevy 4X4 that was screeching to a stop. When both the truck and I stopped, my face was two inches away from the centre of its bumper. I was so close I could see my reflection in the chrome.

For some reason, I wasn't affected personally with any fear or dread; in fact, I was the calmest one standing in the middle of that highway that day. I pulled my dirt bike off the road and got the traffic moving again. After giving my insurance information to the driver of the Camaro and convincing him that we didn't need to call the police, I checked my bike for damage. It was good to go, so I crossed the road and approached the hill that, just minutes before, had gotten the best of me. I tore up that hill with a vengeance and rode down the trails into the woods.

My older brother, Larry, had been riding the other dirt bike, and we stopped on the trail soon to discuss what had happened only moments before. At that time, I gave some serious thought to the validity of what my girlfriend had been telling me. I remember saying to Larry, "It sort of makes you believe in God, doesn't it?" I estimated that the average speed of the cars on that stretch of highway would have been going 90 kilometres per hour; and travelling at that speed, a car covers 82 feet per second. With that in mind, if I had entered the highway a second earlier, I would have been hit by the car in the closest lane. I would have probably kept going and been run over by the Camaro in the far lane; and a second later, the big Chevy 4X4 would have likely run right over me and spit me out the back. Either way, it would have cost me either my life or some serious pain at the very least.

What Was at Play?

Remember that I said I was in a battle and didn't even know it, and that it was seemingly a battle over my eternal soul?

Did one side want to snatch me away before I could finish comprehending and act upon the answers that were being revealed to me about God, about my soul, and about where I would end up for eternity? Or did God, out of His grace, knowing that I was on the fence, give me the push that I needed to make a decision as to whom I was going to put my trust in for my eternal soul? I felt it was time; I didn't believe I'd have chance after chance, and it seemed to me that making no decision at this point would be giving an absolute "no" to God.

Simply put, I was face-to-face with the decision to accept or reject the answers to the questions that I had asked so many years before. Glimpses of my near-death experiences were flashing into my mind's eye; I could clearly see that something was working in my life, and that these situations in my life were pushing me to accept the answers that were set before me.

I had always believed in God and thought I was a good person or at least better than most. I thought that if I were to die, the scales would tip in my favour, and God would let me into His Heaven. I was being shown very clearly that this was not the case.

A month or so after my close call on the dirt bike, I was still reading the intriguing book my girlfriend had given me called *The Late Great Planet Earth.* I was at the part in the book that explained how to have a right relationship with God when it just clicked; my eyes opened to the fact that if I wanted a relationship with God, I had to go through Jesus Christ. This revelation was made clear in my mind when I related it to going to the unemployment office the day before because I needed to see someone about a claim I had made. I knew the person that I needed to see and proceeded to walk back to his office. I walked only a few feet before the receptionist at the front desk stopped me and informed me sternly that I just couldn't do whatever I wanted, and that I had to follow the proper channels. At that moment, thinking about the events from the day before, it all came together. Jesus Christ was "the proper channel": *"Jesus answered, "I am the way and the truth and the life. No one comes to the Father except through me"* (**John 14:6**).

The Deciding Factor

Then God gave me the final push I needed by having me recall another time when my life was held in the balance. Having grown up at the beach as a young boy, I was a good swimmer. This particular day, I was a skinny-nineteen-year old who weighed around one hundred and thirty-five pounds, and my lack of body fat made floating very difficult. Still, I decided to swim out to the fishing nets, as I had done many times over the years. The problem was that I hadn't been swimming in quite a while, and other than working, I wasn't doing any exercising. So, I was a little out of shape for what I planned to attempt.

Off I went without telling anyone my plans; I just got into the water and started to swim to the first fishnet's buoy that was half a kilometre away. The buoy was quite flimsy: just a flag on a stick which was stuck onto an oversized juice can, but it was enough to prop me up—at least, it used to prop me up. When I was around twelve or thirteen, I used these little buoys to hold me up out of the water, so I could rest before swimming back to shore.

Now, at nineteen, I soon realized that the buoy would not support me and that I hadn't considered how far this buoy was from shore and how out of shape I was for this little swim. So, there I was, clutching a buoy that was not keeping me afloat, with exhaustion creeping into my arms and legs. To tell you the truth, I was a little worried.

I looked around at the boats that were cruising by on the beautiful, blue waters of Lake Huron. My pride and reluctance to be embarrassed prevented me from yelling for help; in my mind, I had no other option except to swim back to shore. About fifteen feet away from the buoy, I panicked and my arms began flailing uncontrollably. Within a split second, I was three feet under the surface of the water, looking up.

I regained my composure, but I knew that with my next breath, this could become my watery tomb. No one was there to reach down to save me, and not one person even knew the incredible danger I faced. I was totally alone, and my life was hanging in the balance.

Surprisingly, a feeling of tranquility came over me. I looked at the bottom of the lake and saw ripples in the sandy bottom, and as I looked around, it was as if I were in a big underground aquarium. Above me, sunlight glistened off the top of the water; the scene was so peaceful, it was almost as if it were calling me to stay. Thankfully, I quickly snapped out of it, swam to the surface, flipped onto my back, and started the very slow trek back to shore.

When I broke the surface of the lake, I could barely keep my face above the water; all I could do was swallow the water that splashed into my mouth. My arms and legs were so tired, that I was amazed they worked at all. I could hear the boat propellers buzzing as they passed by, and despite the serious situation I was in, my inconceivable pride kept me from calling out for help.

How stupid was it that I was willing to drown before I would call for help and embarrass myself? In the end, pure determination got me back to shore. Remembering that near-drowning experience taught me something about myself: I had way too much pride.

As I reflected on events from my past, it was obvious to me that I was letting my pride condemn me to hell. That was very evident when I almost drowned and didn't call out for help to the boats passing by, or when I lost control of my dirt bike and slid between the cars on the highway and didn't call out to God immediately for salvation. From my girlfriend's viewpoint, which she shared with me a few times—I was going to Hell, not Heaven.

I knew that my life could have been over in an instant in both cases. My brother Steve's life was over in an instant, with no warning, and this reminiscing over my past was really causing me to think about dealing with my own mortality sooner rather than later. In reality, no one knows when his or her time here on earth is up, and I started to wonder if my next brush with death would be my last.

Clearly, I had been given the answers to all the questions I had asked over the years, and it was decision time: simply put, it came right down to either accepting or rejecting God. It was a decision with consequences that would last for eternity, and God gave me the free will to make that decision any way I chose. But I was also very aware that not making a decision would be considered a rejection on my part.

As I thought about what to do, God brought to mind my experience at the unemployment office on following *the proper channels* and those close calls with death, which put everything into perspective. Jesus Christ was the only way to God, which was foundational for salvation, and **now** was the time to act.

I wanted an answer to the question "Why?" and the answer God gave me was Jesus Christ. I accepted this wholeheartedly by praying from my heart and giving my life to Him. I believed that Christ, being God, allowed Himself to be sacrificed on the cross to clear my debt of sin, saving me from judgement. With that, I invited Jesus to take away my sin which separated me from God and made Jesus Lord of my life. By doing this, I was forgiven by God's merciful grace and received the peace with Him that I sought. It was a simple prayer, but God always hears a prayer from the heart. Amazingly enough, God had been preparing me to say that prayer ever since I had prayed to Him when I was twelve years old.

At this point, the dynamics of the relationship between God and me changed dramatically—it became very personal. I would find myself talking to Jesus as I would a good friend throughout the day. I felt strongly that prayers that had seemed to float into nothingness before were being heard, and not only heard, but I saw them being answered.

At the time, I couldn't even imagine what effect receiving Jesus' forgiveness would have on my life or on my future, but since I received Him, I was motivated for doing what was right and good in His sight...not in any way to work my way to Heaven, but out of gratitude for His gift that now gives me access to Heaven.

I was learning a new value system from God, a value system that my old acquaintances didn't understand and were prone to ridicule me for. But I found answers in the Bible that refuted their comments. Now I was finding it easier to stand on principles, like telling the truth in all circumstances, not swearing, or thinking of others before myself, to mention a few. I thought these principles were lost in this world, but amazingly enough, they began to become a part of who I was.

Another benefit of accepting Jesus' forgiveness was that the Holy Spirit took up permanent residence in me. The Holy Spirit is a gift from God to the believer. His job is to help the believer understand Scripture, awaken us to sin that needs to be dealt with, and guide us to become more like Christ. With the assistance of the Holy Spirit, I was able to comprehend and believe the answers to questions that I sought so many years before.

Jesus became such a vital friend: someone I could count on beyond what I could possibly imagine and someone who treated me in a manner that no one had ever treated me before or has ever been able to do so since. It was a good decision to embrace His friendship and what He had to offer. My side of the friendship could offer nothing other than myself, but that is all He asked and wanted.

Why did I have to believe in Jesus only to be accepted into Heaven, instead of relying on keeping the Ten Commandments?

The Bible is very clear that no one will enter into Heaven by keeping the Ten Commandments. I know this is a strange doctrine for many, but the Ten Commandments were never intended to show us how good we could be: in fact, they were created for the opposite reason: to show us how good we are not. The Ten Commandments, also known as the Laws of God, were only created to bring us to the realization that we were sinners, unable to keep the law which, in turn, keeps us separated from God. Let me explain from God's Word, starting with **Romans 3:20:** *"Therefore no one will be declared righteous in his sight by observing the law; rather, through the law we become conscious (aware) of sin."* The wording here is very concise: by the law, we are sinners, and the Bible describes sinner as helpless and drowning, unable to save themselves. *"I am drowning in the flood of my sins; they are a burden too heavy to bear"* **(Psalm 38:4).**

The Ten Commandments aren't a life preserver to the drowning, but a millstone of great weight. What a stark contrast to what many people think the Ten Commandments' purpose is.

So, if keeping the Ten Commandments isn't going to open Heaven's gate, then how do we?

The answer to the above question is by being justified by faith in Jesus Christ, and not by the law. Justification means we are forgiven, so when God looks at us, He doesn't see our sin, He sees Jesus' righteousness. This concept of law versus faith is explained in **Galatians 2:16:**

> *"Know that a man is not justified by observing the law, but by faith in Jesus Christ. So we, too, have put our faith in Christ Jesus that we may be justified by faith in Christ and not by observing the law, because by observing the law no one will be justified."*

Again, all the Ten Commandments were for is to show us that we are sinful and in need of a Saviour. The following verses tell us precisely what we are, "sinners", and if we could enter Heaven by keeping the Ten Commandments, Christ died a horrible death for nothing.

> *"Therefore, just as sin entered the world through one man (Adam and Eve) and death through sin, and in this way death came to all men, because all have sinned."* – **Romans 5:12**

> *"For all have sinned and fall short of the glory of God."* – **Romans 3:24**

> *"I do not set aside the grace of God, for if righteousness could be gained through the law, Christ died for nothing."* – **Galatians 3:21**

Now some good news: God offers us the gift of salvation through His Son.

"For God so loved the world that he gave his one and only Son, that whoever believes in him shall not perish but have eternal life." – **John 3:16**

"This is love: not that we loved God, but that he loved us and sent his Son as an atoning sacrifice for our sins." – **1 John 4:10**

The Bible is a book about God's nature. God is love; God showed His love towards us in sending His Son to be the ultimate sacrifice (offering) and atonement (payment) for our sins. Nothing other than Christ's atoning sacrifice is needed for our salvation to be complete. **John 19:30** verifies the completeness of that sacrifice: *"When he had received the drink, Jesus said, 'It is finished.' With that, he bowed his head and gave up his spirit."* When Jesus said, "It is finished" and gave up His spirit, His work on the cross was done—His work to redeem (rescue) us from Hell was complete. Faith is the only contribution that is required by anyone seeking Heaven. For many, the simplicity of only having faith in Christ and nothing more is hard to grasp.

But our sins equal a debt that we can never repay. The debt of sin can't be written off; it can't be wiped out by declaring bankruptcy. The payment that is demanded for the sins that we hide in our hearts is eternity in a place that is like a dungeon: a windowless, overwhelmingly dark place where there will never be any other human contact. The thought of being sent to a place of total isolation scared me enough to call out to God so that my debt could be removed.

I am so thankful that there was someone willing to sacrifice His life to pay that debt for me, so that I could be **redeemed** by

His **sacrificial** payment. Who was that person? Jesus Christ, whose sacrificial payment wasn't just for me, but for anyone who is willing to believe. This action of the sinless Christ, dying for the sinful, is called atonement—which is the act of making amends for our sins.

And that is exactly what Jesus did:

> *"You see, at just the right time, when we were still powerless (to save ourselves), Christ died for the ungodly (the sinner). Very rarely will anyone die for a righteous person, though for a good person someone might possibly dare to die. But God demonstrates His own love for in this: While we were still sinners, Christ died for us."* **– Romans 5:8**

So, when we talk about Christ's sacrifice to **redeem** us and the **atonement** (payment) for our sins, it means that He paid the debt that we could never pay. He paid a debt that wasn't His, and He did this loving act because He wanted to do the will of His loving Father. Jesus is the friend in **John 15:13:** *"Greater love has no one than this: to lay down one's life for one's friends."*

The Book of Romans: Death to Life

The verses below clearly show: 1) Sin equals death; 2) God's love for us is evident through Christ's sacrifice; 3) Salvation is a gift—which is achieved by believing from your heart and calling on the name of the Lord.

"For the wages of sin is death, but the gift of God is eternal life in Christ Jesus our Lord." – **Romans 6:23**

"But God demonstrates his own love for us in this: While we were still sinners, Christ died for us." – **Romans 5:8**

"For, everyone who calls on the name of the Lord will be saved." – **Romans 10:13**

"That if you confess with your mouth, Jesus is Lord, and believe in your heart that God raised Him from the dead, you will be saved. For it is with your heart that you believe and are justified and it is with your mouth that you confess and are saved." (from eternity in Hell) – **Romans 10:9–10**

Another benefit of asking to receive Jesus' forgiveness is that, at the moment my prayer was completed, I was adopted into His family, forever. I didn't know the scope of what this entailed at the time, but I knew it was going to be good. Now, after almost forty years of following Christ, I know beyond a shadow of a doubt that my life has been more peaceful and straight because of my faith. It hasn't always been easy because of my prideful nature, and I haven't always walked as close to the Lord as I should have, but He has never revoked my adoption into his family because I went astray; and He never will. Whenever I have moved away from Him by making selfish decisions, He has always drawn me back. In these uncertain times, I am so thankful for my personal walk with Jesus Christ and His unfailing love towards me.

Could you be rejecting Christ and not even know it? The Gospel of **John 3:35–36** says, *"The Father loves the Son and has placed everything in his hands. Whoever believes in the Son has eternal life, but whoever rejects the Son will not see life, for God's wrath remains on them."*

It's that simple: receive the Son, and you have a new life; reject the Son, and that equals spiritual death/punishment. The end of the verse in **John 3:36** is hard to accept for many people, as they are convinced, like I once was, that this part of the verse— *"but whoever rejects the Son will not see life, for God's wrath remains on them"*—is not referring to them. They don't believe that they have rejected the Son (Jesus Christ), even though their lifestyle indicated otherwise, as mine did. It's just easier to turn a blind eye to verses like **John 3:36** and believe the myth that all roads lead to Heaven as long as you believe in something. Having a blind eye is not going to change the fact that God is very adamant—it does matter in whom and in what you place your faith for eternal life.

The best verses in the Bible to encompass the whole of the Gospels is **Ephesians 2:8–9:** *"For it is by Grace you have been saved, through faith—and this not from yourselves, it is the gift of God—not by works, so that no one can boast."*

One: Ephesians 2:8–9 clearly states that we can be saved only by God's grace (His unmerited mercy). **Two:** His grace can be experienced only through faith in Christ as stated in the first part of **John 3:36:** *"Whoever believes in the Son has eternal* *life."* **Three:** Salvation is a gift, so if we tried to buy it or work for it, it's no longer a gift, and the offer becomes void. **Four:** There can be no boasting about getting a gift that God makes absolutely clear we don't deserve.

One of my favourite verses below is a promise for all who have placed their faith solely in Jesus Christ for eternal life.

> *"I (Jesus) give them eternal life, and they shall never perish; no one will snatch them out of my hand. My Father, who has given them to me, is greater than all; no one can snatch them out of my Father's hand. I and the Father are one."* **– John 10:28–30**

In many places in the Gospels, Christ tells us that when we place our trust solely in Him by faith, we will have eternal life; and no one can snatch that away. The imagery in **John 10:28–30** is Christ's holding the believer in His hand, then God the Father's hand is wrapped around Christ's hand. Nothing in Heaven or on earth is going to separate us from God's love and eternal salvation with a grip like that holding us.

3

MY JOURNEY

Who Is the God Behind My Journey—Jesus, the Image of the Invisible God

For my testimony to make sense, one must have an in-depth understanding of why a Saviour is needed and why Jesus Christ, who is the representation in the flesh of the invisible God, is the only one able to fulfill that role. In the following pages, I will share some Bible verses to validate that statement. I will also share some of my personal experiences about my relationship with Jesus Christ.

To have a personal relationship with Jesus Christ, it's imperative to understand who the Bible says He is. I am no Biblical scholar by any means, but over the years, some of the things that I have learned may help to bring some clarity to those who are questioning who the Bible says God is. Many misconceptions exist about God, Heaven, and Hell. Nobody should make an important decision on where one spends eternity based on anything other than searching out God's Word for the answers.

In this book, I will review many of the verses I've already given, but in a bit more detail. I will also draw from my own life experiences to help give a clear overview of who God is and the salvation He freely offers through Jesus Christ.

I do use a number of illustrations in different ways to hammer home important truths, and I revisit those truths throughout the writings many times; bear with me to the end to grasp the significance of the text, and I believe you will see why.

As you read on, please don't skim over any of the Bible verses that are written in this book, even if you are familiar with them. The Holy Spirit uses what's written in the Bible to help us understand the things of God. That's why the Bible is called God's Living Word, because no matter how many times a passage or verse is read, it can still touch one's heart in a new way.

Salvation Is at God's Expense

God offers salvation to mankind as a free gift, and we will never be able to fully grasp the cost of Christ's suffering on the cross for our salvation this side of Heaven. God has given everything through Christ, and if you get to know Him, you will see that there has never been a truer statement. So, I encourage you to take the time to read this through and process the information thoroughly. I pray for all who read this that the Holy Spirit will give understanding to God's words as presented here from the Bible.

As with anything in life, there is a progression, even to God.

- **One:** I needed to see the effect sin was having in my life.

- **Two:** I needed to understand how sin was keeping me from a relationship with God.

- **Three:** I needed to know who *the God of the Bible* really was.

- **Four:** I needed to accept the good news of the Gospels.

- **Five:** I needed to accept Christ into my heart, to have forgiveness of my sin.

- **Six:** I needed to learn to grow to be more like Christ in every aspect of my life.

Why Did I Come to Christ?

Simply put, I didn't want to fall under judgement.

Some come to Christ for that reason, while others come to Christ because they want to know and experience the love of God in their lives. The phrase "I love you" wasn't very common in our household back in the sixties, so searching out God for love wasn't in my nature. Instead, searching out God to escape judgement was. I felt that way as a result of my upbringing; when I was growing up, the last thing I wanted to do was be on my father's bad side. I considered him harsh, and his very judgmental spirit towards me left me feeling that if I screwed up, I was a screwup. (To be fair, this was my perception of my father growing up, and I had limited knowledge of who he really was. On the other hand, my brothers' perception of him could have been totally different, and as you'll see in the following paragraphs, I did make peace with him.)

As a teenager, the fear of judgement and punishment didn't stop me from doing wrong; it just made me better at not getting caught. But with God, getting better at not getting caught isn't an option. For God knows all:

> *"He knows about everyone, everywhere. Everything about us is bare and wide open to the all-seeing eyes of our God; nothing can be hidden from Him to whom we must explain all we have done." – Hebrews 4:13*

Since not getting caught wasn't an option with God, He used this ingrained fear of punishment that my father had instilled in me to show me in my twenties that I was not in good standing in His sight. Basically, in God's eyes, I was under judgement for my sinfulness, and not wanting to die in that state is what drew me to Him for forgiveness.

My experiences with my earthly father were skewing my view of my Heavenly Father's love towards me. Looking back, I can't remember doing a lot with my father growing up: we didn't have much in common, I did not share his love of golf, and I didn't think he even liked me that much. A father-child bond of love wasn't nurtured. For as long as I can remember, he spent most of his time at the golf course; and in later years, he and my mom spent their winters down in Florida. We really didn't have a tight family life; living for oneself was more the norm. I was no better at living for others than anyone else in my family until God got a hold of my life in the early 1980s. Even to this day, I struggle with personal selfishness.

That's why I had such a hard time when I first came to Christ; my view of my Heavenly Father was too intertwined with my view of my earthly father. Over the years, though, through studying the Bible and being mentored by men of God who showed the love of God the Father in a positive light, I came to understand what the Bible meant when it described how God loves each one of us on this earth. Embracing God's love, I didn't see Him as judgmental anymore—He wasn't waiting for me to screw up so He could reprimand me—but showed His love towards me through the sacrifice of His Son on the cross for my salvation. After accepting that sacrificial gift, I was adopted into God's family as His own. I was privileged to receive all God had to offer: His grace, His compassion, the indwelling of the Holy Spirit and, when my time here on earth is up, Heaven. Being adopted into God's family gave me a true sense of belonging; Jesus Christ became my protector, encourager, friend, comforter, helper, teacher, and an example of how to live in God's righteousness.

Whether you fear God's judgement or are drawn by the love of God—or for any other reason—I don't think there is a right or a wrong way to come to Jesus as long as you come and accept His offer of grace. After acceptance, getting to know God in His entirety through a relationship established by believing in Jesus Christ is a journey of faith. As with any relationship, a person's connection of kinship with God takes time and effort to grow; but as your relationship with God grows, His love and compassion for all of the human race becomes apparent. When I learned this, I no longer lived in fear of screwing up, but experienced God's forgiveness and gentleness working through my imperfections and mistakes. Through accepting Jesus into my heart, I now viewed God as my loving heavenly Father.

How Connecting with My Dad Came About

It wasn't until the later years of my father's life that I actually got to know my dad; how this came about was because of his hands. He had what is called Dupuytren's Contracture, a disease which causes the fingers to pull in towards the palm. Over time, the disease makes it impossible for the affected person's fingers to straighten, so the hands stay in a fist-like position. I know from personal experience with Dupuytren's Contracture in my own hands how very uncomfortable this debilitating disease is. For my father, this disease took away his passion for golf. Looking back, I am impressed that with all this disease took away, and with all the physical pain it caused—I know how painful it can be at times—I never heard him complain. It was a growing insight into his character.

When my dad couldn't play golf anymore, I was the one who became blessed; instead of my father being on the golf course on Sunday mornings, he and I began to pick up a couple of Tim Horton's double-double coffees, drive to Point Edward, and park under the Bluewater Bridge in my big, green Starcraft Conversion van. Those warm Sunday mornings throughout the summer—with the wind gently carrying the fresh smell of Lake Huron through our open windows, watching the St. Clair River flowing by, talking to my dad about things he had never shared before—were awesome. For the first time in my life, I got to really know my dad, which dispelled some of the childhood hurts I still had towards him. My dad didn't become perfect, but seeing him in a different light sure made forgiveness easier.

Seeing Similarities Between My Dad and Myself

Now, when my dad shared stories about his youth and gave his views on many different things, I felt that I was more like an equal than a kid who should be seen and not heard. I think many households in the sixties held the view that kids should be seen and not heard; it was the mantra for both parents and children. So, his treating me as an equal was a big deal to me.

It's funny; over the years, I tried so hard to win my dad's approval, but I felt I was never able to hit the mark. I also brought this attitude of trying to win approval into my Christian life with God the Father for a long time. It amazes me how wrapped up my perception of my Heavenly Father was with that of my earthly father. It took a while, but I learned that God sees me as perfect through Jesus Christ. I don't have to prove myself to God; I just have to let His Spirit work through me to become more like Christ.

I was more like my dad than I thought, and this became very apparent when my daughter-in-law made a comment about how my eldest son was always looking for my approval, much the same way that I was always looking for my own father's approval. I thought I was better at showing approval to my kids than my dad, but I guess not.

I learnt firsthand in the summer of 2020 how poorly I handed out praise and how easily I could criticize a job that was done well. My wife and I own a cottage near Bayfield. My son, his wife, and our three grandkids were staying at the cottage for a week while they were home from Edmonton on vacation. That summer, our shoreline was being destroyed by high water levels; the waves were hitting farther up on shore than ever before. To fight this erosion, we purchased large, heavy wire cages that held good-sized rocks to put along the shoreline. These cages were called gabion bails. These bails were delivered flat and had to be assembled by wiring the sides and top together to make the cage. Each bail took a couple of hours to assemble and was very tedious work.

Before we left for home after enjoying the weekend with them, I asked Oliver, my oldest son, to do me a favour. He said that he would be more than happy to help, for they were going to be the only ones up there for the week. I asked him if he would assemble ten gabion bails for me. He told me that that would be no problem. I showed him exactly how I wanted them assembled, and we left for home.

When my wife and I arrived at the cottage the following weekend, the first thing I did was inspect the job that I had given him. He could have done a hundred things right, but I probably picked on anything that wasn't done how I would have done it. I had become my dad. This brought back to mind when I would hear my kids jokingly say at times among themselves, "You can never please Dad." I pray that my shortcoming in the area of praise towards them didn't give them a poor image of their Heavenly Father like I once had.

Growing up, I didn't receive a lot of praise from my father for things I had done, correction was more of the norm. As an adult, I just loved it when I heard my father talking to someone and boast about me for something I did that he was proud of. Amazingly enough, even though I was a grown man, it made me feel ten feet tall. If a little boasting from my father made such a difference in how I felt, you would think that I would be boasting about my kids in front of them all the time. Unfortunately, it's the opposite, but it shouldn't be.

I guess they're always going to be kids in my eyes to some degree. I know this was the case with my dad and me. I see my kids (who are now all in their thirties) as still a little helpless without me. I guess you never lose that parental component or the need to feel needed by your kids.

My Dad's Story

My dad grew up during the Great Depression of the 1930's in Galt, Ontario. He was the youngest by many years and what some would call the "oops baby". He was not one to sit around and tell stories, so I don't know much about his childhood, but I do remember his exaggerated stories that always began with "when I was growing up," followed by an explanation of how he walked to school ten miles each way, uphill in both directions, in a blizzard. My dad's family were not as bad off as many at that time, for Grandpa had a good job as a machinist. It wasn't until the summer of 2005, I think, that I learned anything about my dad's childhood, youth, and war experiences.

Listening to stories Dad told about growing up, I sensed an underlying thread of harshness when he talked about his father— not that he spoke of him that much. I got the sense that there weren't many hugs and proclamations of "I love you" in his childhood home, and I concluded that my dad was a product of his era. His dad was harsh and just doing the best he could. I imagine my dad's grandfather was also a harsh man, and this is what was handed down through the generations. Understanding this, I realized that my dad's character really was an improvement over his father's and grandfather's characters, and probably over all the generations before.

I am not judging my ancestors, for they lived in a time where the issues of life were so different. We think about what we're going to have for dinner; they thought about how they were going to put food on the table. We think about what we're going to wear; they thought about having something to wear. We think about how big a house and in what neighbourhood we want to live; they thought about how to put a roof over their heads. The list could go on and on. The point here is not to disrespect those from the past but to understand where certain traits come from and why.

Listening to my dad talk about the war showed me more insight into his character: he lied about his age to join the army and explained that he joined because all of his friends were joining. He also said that his time serving in World War Two was the greatest experience of his life. But he was also a modest man. My mother once told us of a time when my father helped a fellow soldier who was badly hurt. As she put it, he carried that man farther than humanly possible until he came across others who were able to get him to safety. My mom told my dad that he should have told someone—that he would have gotten a medal for his bravery, but he responded that it was just what you did: you helped those who needed help in the same way they helped you. My dad was shot in the war; the bullet went right through him in the upper stomach without damaging any major organs. He then spent six weeks convalescing in the hospital and was sent back up to the front. We'd never have known if it hadn't been for my mom.

As we watched the river flow by on those precious Sunday mornings, and he shared a coffee and his reminiscences about his World War Two experiences with me, my view of him changed dramatically. I saw him in a totally different light; I felt a deep respect towards him, washing away my past resentment.

My dad didn't share his life with us as a family very much, and what has been said is all that we have. That generation has all passed away, forever burying their history in the cemetery. What a contrast to the life of Jesus Christ; all we need to know about Him and God is written in the Bible for all to know. As I read through the Scriptures, I personally got to know God, and I came to see him in a totally different light: He was not a God waiting to bring down fire and brimstone on my head, but a God of mercy and grace through Jesus Christ.

Getting to Know My Heavenly Father

As I said, my view of my earthly father changed dramatically as I got to know him. This was also true when I discovered what my Heavenly Father was like. Through Bible reading and prayer, my harsh impression of Him changed dramatically as well. In both cases, I went from an attitude of fearfulness to a healthy respect.

In light of all that I had learned about my dad, it was easy for me to forgive him for his shortcomings as a father. How could I not? He had done the best he could with the life experiences he had and what was handed down from his father. It's just a little sad that it wasn't until the last years of his life that I was able to reconcile my feelings towards him.

In the same way, taking the time to find out who my dad was, which led to reconciliation, was similar to taking the time to find out who God was; doing that dispelled the wrong information I had about Him, which led me to be reconciled to Him through Jesus Christ. One thing that I have learned is this: to have a good relationship with anyone, you have to find out who they are, what they think, how they feel, and how they love. Acquiring or acting on wrong perceptions about God, or anyone else for that matter, is the fault of the person not taking the time to find out the truth. Superficial relationships require little effort, but meaningful relationships, on the other hand, require hard work from both parties, which can be a little overwhelming, but worth it.

My dad and I didn't seem to put much effort into our father and son relationship when I was growing up; he was hard to approach, and I had a big chip on my shoulder. But like I said, he was doing the best he could—for his teaching on how to display love was somewhat lacking in his childhood. I came to be okay with the fact that my dad wasn't perfect in showing his love, but I knew he did love me, and that was enough.

Neither my dad nor I changed overnight, but our relationship did grow to where we were able to talk a little bit more about things that mattered, even to the point of talking about spiritual things. These talks about the things of God softened his heart to where his grandson, Oliver, was able to lead him to the Lord before he passed on. Because of Jesus, I have the promise I will see my dad again in Heaven when my time comes.

I am so glad my relationship with my Heavenly Father wasn't as hard to figure out as many of the human relationships I have had. I think the fact that God demonstrates perfect love towards us has everything to do with the ease in which a relationship with Him grows.

Perfect love is only from God, but you would think since love has always been the better part of our human existence, the meaning and demonstration of love wouldn't be so hard.

The question is: If God is love—why is there a stipulation on getting into Heaven? The answer to that question has to do with sin.

God's love for us can't override His righteousness; if He didn't deal with sin according to His sinless nature, His holiness would be compromised, and in fact, God wouldn't be holy at all. Being holy is the attribute of God that binds all the other attributes together: His love, justice, grace, mercy (which is the only thing that can spare us from Hell), goodness, faithfulness, unchanging wisdom, unchanging nature, and never-ending self-sufficiency and power. He is the infinite God.

Since all the attributes of God have to be in harmony, God won't override His holiness and justice to overlook our sinful state. His justice demands sin to be dealt with before anyone can enter Heaven, and that's the only stipulation on entering.

No one attribute of God is more important than the other, but we must keep them in balance in how we relate to Him. You can't pick the attributes of God that you like and disregard the rest. God is a God of love, but also a God of justice, and for the justice to be satisfied concerning sin, He sent His Son Jesus Christ to the cross on our behalf to be our Saviour.

- **What is a Saviour?** A person who saves someone or something from danger or difficulty.

- **Why do we need a Saviour?** Because God's **prescribed** punishment for **sin** is death (separation).

- **What does God call sin?** It is anything that goes against His nature in act, deed, word or thought.

- **The Bible's definition of sin is straightforward:** rebellion or disobedience against God, ingratitude, or a lack of appreciation for all that God has given us, and not glorifying or lifting up God for who He is.

Romans 1:21 says:

"Yes, they knew God, but they wouldn't worship him as God or even give him thanks. And they began to think up foolish ideas of what God was like. As a result, their minds became dark and confused."

Doesn't **Romans 1:21** sum up what today's world thinks about God. If you ask people if there is a God, most will probably say "yes." Ask them to describe God, and you would get a wide range of answers. I think most would say God is love, but not too many would say God is a God that would send anyone to Hell, even though the Bible is very clear on God's righteousness, judgements, Heaven, and Hell.

God's Word was written by men, who were influenced by the Holy Spirit to write exactly what God wanted them to write with no mistakes, no improvisations, no contradictions—just God's Holy words accurately written out in one book.

What ramification do you think there could be by not considering what is written in the Bible as true? I urge you to read on and draw your own conclusions.

4

FREE WILL AND LOVE

You cannot have true love without the freedom of the **will.** Free will gives us the opportunity to love freely. I am not talking about some of the crazy ideas people have about love in some elements of society today, or the short-term, ooey-gooey love feelings at the start of a relationship, or the selfish one-way love which seems to influence a lot of today's relationships. No, I am talking about imitating God's way of loving with His virtue, showing compassion, keeping promises, selflessness, putting others above yourself, respecting and valuing others, and protecting the very sanctity of love and life. That is what true love is supposed to look like.

Also, freedom is indispensable to love, and God's supreme goal for you and me is that we will love him with all our hearts and love our neighbours as ourselves. For him to violate our free will removes the necessary component for love to flourish and be freely expressed.

Ultimately, the choice we make for eternity is made by the submission of our will to our heavenly Father. He will not violate our will. **That freedom is given to us by Him.**

Love Is an Act of the Will, Not Just a Feeling

A preacher friend once said, "Love is not a feeling; it's an act of the will. If you fall out of love, will yourself back into love." That has been the truest statement I have ever heard, and many times over the years, I have done exactly that: willed myself back into love. Many distractions come with the busyness of life, and those distractions can sever a loving relationship. Add in selfishness, and the heart can grow cold. When this comes to light, an act of will is needed to get up and resume the job of loving again. If we are going to love someone or follow God only by feelings alone, what a bumpy ride that will be. At the first sign of turbulence in either relationship, out the door we go. Just because we have the freedom to leave when things get rough doesn't mean that we should. Taking the easy way out disregards the fact that freedom should equal responsibility: to work at a marriage, to work at following and serving God, and to work at making proper decisions that benefit others and ourselves for good.

Any freedom that this world has ever achieved has always come at the cost of great human suffering. Spiritual freedom is no different; it was bought by Jesus' suffering on the cross. The difference between spiritual freedom and the world's freedom is that it can be very short-lived, and history has proven that many times over, whereas spiritual freedom offered by Jesus Christ is everlasting.

When it comes to our freedoms, if not used wisely, freedom to choose how we live and how we act can cause many problems. Our society today disregards God and His teaching on many levels, deeming it outdated and irrelevant. Everyone seems to be going in his or her own direction, and this causes much havoc throughout the world. I have heard this comment more than once: "What's wrong with the world today?" Many say if God was a loving God, then why are things so out of control? If we were following God's precepts (rules) to the letter and then things went south, only then could we take issue with Him over the state of the world; however, shaking an angry fist and blaming Him for our inability to do what is ethical just doesn't seem right.

The ones that shake an angry fist at God are able to do so only because God gives all of mankind the freedom to exercise his or her free will. But the result of using that free will not to worship God is laid out in **Romans 1:21**, which says, *"Yes, they knew God, but they wouldn't worship him as God or even give him thanks. And they began to think up foolish ideas of what God was like. As a result, their minds became dark and confused."* So, we can use our free will anyway we choose, but as I have found in my life, choosing God's will over my will brought peace, direction, and meaning into my life. But what about those who refuse to honour God? In his book, *The Great Divorce*, C.S Lewis says there are two kinds of people in this world: "those who bend their knee and say to God, 'Your will be done' or those who refuse to bend their knee to God, and God says to him (or her), 'your will be done.'"[ii] And we can all see what following our own will has done in this world.

You can say, "Mike it's not that bad; you're being negative or pessimistic." Yes, and that is easy to do. Just watching the news makes me that way. But the point is—imagine if everyone followed God's will in *"Love your neighbour as yourself."* What a transformation that would be. Crime, world hunger, weapons of war, and many other hurtful things would be non-existent. So, is it God's fault or ours for the way things are?

Free will, when not used properly, can cause problems. What would it look like if God restrained our free will, seemingly for the benefit of others? Whose free will would be restricted the most? Remember, we would not see the other side of the coin. We wouldn't know what that person was going to do before his or her free will was taken from them. In the same way, the mistakes we make help us learn. If our free will is restrained because someone may get hurt, the person getting hurt could lose out on learning a valuable lesson on how to forgive, a lesson that will certainly be a benefit their entire life. On the other hand, the person who did the hurting might lose out on learning a very valuable lesson: hurting anyone comes with a cost. And that lesson will also be a benefit their entire life.

Restraining our free will overall would be unfair—yes, it would take the bad out of society, but it would also take away our freedom to do good, removing the will of the spirit. Our spirit motivates us to survive in the face of challenges, to love, to overcome, to be who we are, and to serve God or not. Yes, free will has its negative and positive effects, but we can't be anything more than a robot without it.

Because I love my kids, I have had to let them make mistakes so that they could learn; I have had to let them exercise their free will in order to mature. When they were young, I sometimes had to step in for their own safety or benefit; but when I stepped in when they were older, it just caused problems, and their learning curves were stifled.

No, God did not make robots; he made man with the free will to choose to love and follow Him or not. But free will and our sinful nature have made a mess of things. Why is that? The next chapter on sin gives us a good idea of why.

5

SIN

Is All Sin Equal?

Offending God in act, deed, word, or thought is easier to do than you think because God doesn't gauge sin by its severity.

When we think of the sins that would keep us out of Heaven, we tend to think of, for example, murder, depravity, wickedness, and violence—all terrible sins, to say the least. I just finished reading *The Sunflower* by Simon Wiesenthal. It's about a man who was a prisoner of war in the Nazi concentration camps. I think we can agree that the sins of the Nazi guards were worthy of the judgement of Hell.

But what if the sins that keep us out of Heaven don't have to be that wicked? What if the sins of harshness, anger, greed, pride, or just not acknowledging God for who He is are the sins that could keep us out of Heaven? How would that affect us—

knowing that we don't have to be as wicked as a Nazi working in a concentration camp to be unworthy of eternity in Heaven?

The Bible says sin is sin to a sinless God. If that is true, then we can assume all sin, great or small, carries the same consequences—separation from God.

Many view telling a little white lie for a good reason as okay or harmless. God's view of telling a little white lie, for any reason, is simply that it is lying. Some believe that hate kept to ourselves is not that terrible, but **1 John 3:15** says that those who hate are considered murderers in the eyes of the Lord. Wow, that is a concept rarely embraced, but that is how God defines it.

We must conclude that God's view of sin is very different than ours, and we need to see that sin in the context of how God sees it—grievous. For if we don't, we will just keep fooling ourselves in thinking that we're okay in God's sight when the reality of the situation is that we're not, and that would be a mistake that would have repercussions for eternity.

To get a glimpse of how God sees our personal sin, all we need to do is ask the Holy Spirit to open our eyes. When the Holy Spirit opened my eyes, I saw my sin for what it was—grievous and needing to be dealt with sooner rather than later. That's when I came to God and asked for forgiveness. If you ask the Holy Spirit to open your eyes to sin, the first thing you're going to realize is that you're not as good as you thought, and that is the time to be totally honest with yourself. Honesty with self is not an easy thing to do, but it is the only way to see sin for what it is—a curse to our souls, which should point us to Jesus for salvation. With God, honesty is key.

Honesty—Where Should It Start?

On one occasion, I had a frank conversation with the salesperson where I buy most of my automotive parts for my business. We talked about the level of honesty to which their company wanted me to adhere. This came about when I had ordered a quantity of small washers that we use when changing oil. When the order came in, I counted three more washers than the fifty originally ordered. I promptly called my supplier and asked them to invoice me for the extra three washers. This was amusing to the salesperson, as each washer cost just over ten cents each. In view of how much I purchased from that company each year, the amount of the three washers was incredibly insignificant.

The salesperson told me it was not a big deal and not to worry about it—probably thinking that I was out to lunch or a little too obsessive on the matter. This led me to ask the salesperson an important question: *Where should honesty start— at a thousand dollars?* The salesperson answered, "No". Then I asked if it should be five hundred dollars, and the answer was still no. We played this game until I finally asked, "At what point do you expect me to start being honest?" The reply was, "I invoiced you for the other three washers. Have a nice day."

If I had just kept those three washers without paying for them—by the letter of the law—I would have been stealing. When it comes right down to it, you are either honest or you are not. Honesty has been put on a sliding scale only by today's sinful society. But God's honesty is not on a sliding scale, nor are His views on sin or justice.

From a worldly view, it's really hard to understand how God views the seriousness of sin, especially when the world sees sin on an unbalanced scale tipping in its favour. But one thing I have learned is this: if my sin is not dealt with by receiving Jesus Christ as my Saviour, the predetermined punishment for that sin is a place called Hell. For the scales in God's court are totally balanced, and they are not, nor will they ever be, tipped in the favour of a sinful world.

Out of Place

Why is no sin allowed to enter into Heaven? It would be comparable to a ragged, unwashed, and unclean person who lived on the streets for much of his life showing up at a very prestigious wedding event where black tie and elegant gowns were the requisite attire. If he were mistakenly allowed into the banquet room, he would feel out of place and awkward. He would be vividly aware that, *in his present state*, he did not belong there. The other invited guests would be embarrassed for the ragged person in their midst, and the entire event would be tarnished in a sense. If a sinful person were allowed into Heaven without being made clean by Christ, the same would be true. Heaven would be tainted.

Isaiah 1:18 says:

> *"The Lord says, Now, let's settle the matter. You are stained red with sin, but I will wash you as clean as snow. Although your stains are deep red, you will be as white as wool."*

If everyone in Heaven were as white as wool, a person stained red would not fit in. Sin, specifically all sin, needs to be dealt with before entering Heaven—for our sinful nature would become very evident to us if we were allowed to step into God's environment of sinlessness. Just like the homeless person who didn't see himself as dirty until he was brought into a different environment and a cleaner place, I know that in my life I have been in places where I felt very out of my element and couldn't wait to leave. It's a very uncomfortable feeling being in a place where you don't belong; it's a feeling that I wouldn't want to feel for eternity.

What Is Our Standing Before God, With and Without Christ?

"But, therefore, being justified by faith, we have peace with God through our Lord Jesus Christ" (**Romans 5:1**). With Christ, we can know the will of God; we can conform to His image and are no longer seen as an enemy of God or wicked or sinful, but redeemed. With Christ, we are welcomed into Heaven—God's sinless environment—washed clean of our sins. Our standing before God through Jesus Christ is as His children: worthy to be called sons and daughters, clothed in God's righteousness. No longer are we orphans—destitute and spiritually helpless—but adopted into God's family.

Without Christ, **Billy Graham** puts it this way: "Whether you consider yourself an enemy of God does not matter. It is what God thinks. Because you have rejected His love, His offer of reconciliation, His offer of peace—you are considered an enemy."[iii]

Are you confident that you haven't unknowingly rejected God's love or His offer of peace? Do you feel it is just preposterous to even think you could be an enemy of God or considered wicked in His sight?

That is exactly how I felt; I wasn't perfect, but I was sure that I wasn't God's enemy. I mean, I was a good person as far as the world defines good. So how could I be an enemy?

Truth be told, I was God's enemy for the simple reason— which the Bible addresses repeatedly—that I am a sinner from birth, and my sin has alienated me from a Holy God. No amount of good works or trying to be presentable enough on my own is going to change that. Trusting in myself instead of God's plan for salvation through accepting Jesus Christ's offer of forgiveness is saying to God, "I'm superior, and I know what's best for me." With this prideful thinking, I was unknowingly rejecting His love, His offer of reconciliation, and His offer of peace. I may have done this without really realizing it, but that didn't change my standing in His sight.

Pride makes it easy to think that we're good enough (like I once thought) to stand in God's presence, justified. But the Bible is very clear: everyone without a personal relationship with Jesus Christ is not justified before God, but is considered an adversary—an enemy of God.

You may say, "I know who Jesus is." I also knew who Jesus was, but not in the way it was laid out in the Bible. My thinking wasn't supported by Scripture. I was putting way too much confidence in bits and pieces of truth and hearsay, rather than finding out what the Bible actually said about who Jesus was and the gift of salvation He offers. So, you have to ask yourself whether you are putting your faith in the Jesus of the Bible or a handed-down philosophy, thinking that as long as you believe in something spiritual, everything will work out.

I have learned one very important truth concerning what God says versus what I think: God is never wrong, God is not a man that He should change His mind, and what God thinks is always going to come to pass (paraphrased from **Numbers 23:19**). So, the only discerning thing to do is conform to His will and take Him at His Word.

Note: You can't conform to the will of God if you don't know who the real God is. God is not a pie-in-the-sky ideal. His Word is very clear on how we should come to Him and how we can know His will. We need to follow His instructions to the letter; His teachings are very precise, for He is the One who created us and who gave us a way to know Him personally. Again, I can't stress enough that it doesn't matter what we think; it's what God thinks that counts.

Let's look at it another way. Fugu (pufferfish) is a delicacy throughout Japan, but the tetrodotoxin found in the fish is more toxic than cyanide. Chefs must undergo rigorous training and then take an in-depth exam to legally be allowed to prepare the poisonous pufferfish. If you are in a Japanese restaurant and ordered fugu, would you not want the chef to prepare that fish strictly by the instructions, or would you be okay with having him just wing it?

Think about it: the consequences of not following the instructions on how to properly prepare the pufferfish are similar to not properly following God's instructions. One is instant physical death, while the other is spiritual death—a separation from God for eternity. If the pufferfish is prepared properly, the result is delightful. If the instructions in God's Word are sought out and followed, life has meaning, purpose, and everlasting joy. But neither can be obtained using shortcuts; it is very important to both know and follow the instructions without deviation in both cases. So, please take the time to read on and learn what the Bible says those instructions are.

Let's Get Back to the Problem of Sin

Descriptive words for sin include defilement, corruption, dishonesty, fraudulence, wrongdoing, disobedience, immorality…and the list goes on. Sin has many definitions. It's not the degree of sin that is pertinent; it's that sin is associated with all of mankind in general and attached to our everyday lives one way or another.

How Do You See Yourself Concerning Sin?

Do you see sin attached to your everyday life? Or, are you oblivious to your sin? Or, do you view yourself as a person who sins but is basically good, as someone whose sins aren't that terrible, so you feel that you're okay? Basically, do you view yourself as a person that does the right thing most of the time, totally confident that you're okay with God, and He's okay with you?

I have heard it said that we are all basically good and want to do the right thing. But if this is the norm, then why do we need so many laws to keep people on the straight and narrow? If people, overall, are that good, then why do we lock our cars and houses at night? Why are jails filled to capacity and courts overflowing? In light of this, I have to believe that what the Bible says about man is true: we're basically not that good and are, in fact, sinful. What part of the above statement do you feel describes yourself—basically good or not that good but sinful?

If you are not flawless in the eyes of God, then you fall in the category of **Romans 3:23**, which says, *"For all have sinned and fall short of the glory of God."*

This means that everyone, including you and me, has fallen short of God's standards for righteousness. In fact, no amount of trying to be good or doing good deeds (works) will ever negate our sinfulness; and in our sinful state, we will never obtain the standard of righteousness that is needed to receive God's approval.

The Sin Is Hidden in Our Hearts

Jesus taught in **Matthew 5:27–28,** *"You have heard that it was said, 'You shall not commit adultery.' But I tell you that anyone who looks at a woman lustfully has already committed adultery with her in his heart."*

The same is true concerning unjust anger towards another person. It will be subject to judgement just as if you had murdered that person. God's view of sin is very different than ours; you must understand that we're judged by His perspective of sin and not our own.

The Sin of Omission

"So whoever knows the right thing to do and fails to do it, for him it is sin" **(James 4:17).** I know there have been times in my life when I knew in my heart I should have done the right thing by helping out or giving my time, but I didn't and felt bad for not doing so. Usually, if your conscience convicts you about something, it's probably sin.

Unfortunately, another aspect of sin is the exponential effects. I think Vince Vitale explains this type of sin very well:

> "Sometimes we vastly underestimate our sin and its consequence in this life, and there is also the consequence of us using our free will that affects other people's lives. Let's just say I am harsh to others and put them down, and let's say one of those people becomes so downcast by my actions and the actions of others that they turn to drinking or drugs or maybe even suicide. Also, what would that do in the context of their family? What would that do in the context of future generations to come! It's sobering to think about how our sin can have such far-reaching effects. How is God going to hold me accountable for my involvement if it was in my power to befriend them and build them up, which could have resulted in a different outcome altogether? We always have to remember that God does not look upon sin as we do. His standard is one that we can barely comprehend because everything we view is tainted with our own sinful nature. How do we view our sinful nature? Is it the worst part of us and needs to be dealt with? Or just part

of the human condition and not that big a deal? If viewed as bad and needing to be dealt with, we are more likely to think we're lost and in need of help. If viewed as just the way we are, we definitely won't see ourselves in the light of how God sees us without Christ—sinful and lost—and we may never call out to God for help, or see the effects our sin has had on others. I can look back at my life as a teenager right now and say that I thought at that time some of the things I did were no big deal, but the reality is that they were truly terrible. The standard for our own righteousness shouldn't be seeing someone on the six o'clock news who has done something more horrible than we have and then imparting justification to ourselves because we think we are better than those portrayed on the news. No, the standard for righteousness comes from a holy God. So, try to think what our sin looks like from His perspective, noting that He sees the multiple and the exponential effects of our sin. Maybe Jesus puts this in better perspective in some of His statements—that lust would look like adultery or that unjust anger would look like murder. We have to understand Hell in a relationship framework. Jesus invites us into a relationship with Himself, noting a relationship can be entered into only if both people say yes to that relationship. If we're not willing to say yes to that relationship, then there is nothing Jesus can do on His side; and without a relationship with Jesus, we will not escape judgement. Why is Jesus the only way to

Heaven? Because Jesus is Heaven. That's what Heaven is. Why is Jesus the only way to eternal life? Because Jesus is eternal life. God created you and desires to be friends with you in a flourishing relationship more than anything. That is what eternal life is all about; it is not just some theme park ticket we get: if we decide to use it, that's great, and if we don't, that's okay too. The whole thing is the relationship with God through Christ. If you don't want to be with God, God is not going to force you to be with Him. But being apart from Him in the context of eternity—that's what we call Hell."[iv]

Remember, any sin that we have committed—whether today or anytime in the past that has escaped our memory—are still very vivid in God's eyes; He does not forget. So, who will be found guiltless? I guarantee that it will not be you, me, or anyone else.

Recap: On Sin

Sin is based on our outward actions, inward thoughts, and all the things that we knew we should have done but omitted doing throughout our entire lives. Also, it's based on how our sins affect the lives of others. It's clear—sin completely permeates every area of our lives. This recap would be absolutely devastating if it weren't for the next chapter on God's grace.

6

GOD'S GRACE

Gods's grace, which is His unmerited favour toward us, is not dependent on how good we are or anything we have done; it's totally given freely out of His deep love towards us. It is demonstrated by Jesus going to the cross so that our relationship that was severed by sin can be restored.

Hindrances to Grace

The Good Person Theory is an obstacle to grace. Misunderstanding the Gospel of Grace will result in a religion that is 'works' oriented and is guided by a spirit of self-righteousness. All of which falls short of God's plan for salvation.

Trying to achieve self-righteousness by works equals pride. There are two types of pride. The first is the healthy pride that you feel when you have done a good job or put a lot of effort into something you made. This is the type that makes you step back and admire your work. The second is a self-righteous pride—one that lords accomplishments over others and has an air of superiority. This pride doesn't listen to others, for it always knows better.

As the Bible says in **Proverbs 16:18,** *"Pride goes before destruction, a haughty spirit before a fall."* I know this verse is true, for it has been lived out in my life many times over.

One example of pride is a time when I had completed a difficult and time-consuming engine repair on a motorcycle. Once I finished, I saw how the repair could be done in less time. A fellow worker had a friend that was going to do the same repair. Trying to be helpful, I wrote out the instructions and offered them to him. His response was, "I don't need your help." He let his pride get in the way of accepting my instructions. Later, he apologized for being so arrogant and told me that it would have been a lot easier if he had listened.

The funny thing is, I have repeated that scenario many times over throughout my life, being the guy that doesn't want to listen. For a long time, when it came to having a relationship with God, I didn't want to listen because I knew better—due to my pride. If we desire a relationship with God, we should ditch our pride and take the time to search out what is involved. We need to do this so that we can be sure that the basis of the relationship is in line with God's instructions.

It's also important to take the time to search the Bible to learn who God really is. Many follow a made-up, feel-good god that is basically a god of convenience, called on only when needed. This type of god has no power: no ears to hear, no eyes to see, no voice for comfort or peace. I, on the other hand, want *the God of the Bible*—He who has power, ears to hear, eyes to see, and a voice I can hear to bring comfort, peace, and forgiveness to my soul.

If our choice is a relationship with *the God of the Bible*, again, shouldn't we follow His guidelines on how that relationship should be pursued and lived out? Nowhere in the Bible does it say that we should work our way into God's heart by anything other than accepting His grace by faith and giving ourselves over to His calling through Christ's work on the cross.

Works vs. God's Grace

I know a lot of good people who, based on the Ten Commandments, believe that they are good enough to be let into Heaven. How do I know this? When I ask the question, "Why should God allow you into His Heaven?" the answer is often, "I am not that bad of a person." Then I hear a list of what sins they haven't committed (omitting the ones they have). So, to see where they would spend eternity, how would they stand up if they were on trial for their inward thoughts and outward actions concerning the Ten Commandments? Keep in mind that it's not the degree of the wrongdoing in thoughts or actions, but just that it was done in any shape or form.

This is how the Bible answers that statement: *"Therefore no one will be declared righteous in God's sight by the works of the law (Ten Commandments) rather, through the law we become conscious of our sin"* (**Romans 3:20**).

From the verse above, those good people who try to justify themselves to God by keeping the Ten Commandments are missing the mark. In **Romans 3:20** and many other places in the

Bible, it is clear that the only function of the Ten Commandments is to show us our sinfulness. Hopefully, once we realize that we're sinners and cannot save ourselves, the next step will be to call on God to find forgiveness.

Remember, the Bible says it's "either/or." It can't be both. We either trust our own good works—which leads to continuous separation from God for eternity—or we are totally dependent on God's grace, which leads to forgiveness and eternal life.

Having the view that just being good or doing good things (what the Bible calls *good works*) will be enough to earn us God's favour is nothing new. Some do good works for selfish reasons— like going to church every Sunday for appearance's sake while getting nothing out of the sermon, for their mind is a thousand miles away. Also, some do so-called good works by helping only those who are able to return the favour when needed, but still boast about how they helped someone. Then there are those who do good works for the totally wrong reasons, such as only for recognition and praise—outwardly acting humble while inwardly feeding their pride. These all have the appearances of doing good but are clearly motivated by selfishness.

How will these seemingly good works appear to a God that knows their motives on every little thing they have ever done? Keep in mind that, when standing before God, the question at hand is why God should let you into His Heaven. All good works done with the intent of finding favour with God will be like dirty rags, worthless—and at that point, God will quote from **Matthew 25:41:** *"Then He will say to those on His left, depart from me, you who are cursed, into the eternal fire prepared for the devil* *and his angels.*" Those to whom Jesus says "Depart from Me" are the ones who would not trust only in Him for their salvation, but try to justify themselves by what they are doing; they are trying to make another path to God, other than one He laid out so clearly in His Word, which is faith in only Jesus' work on the cross and nothing else. They may have thought their motives were pure, but God, who knows the true motives of every man's heart, said differently when He told them to "Depart from Me."

There is only one way to Heaven, so don't be deceived by the idea that we can be good enough or do enough good works to earn our way to Heaven, for it's one of Satan's most cunning lies, which mankind has wholeheartedly embraced as truth.

Don't get me wrong: it's commendable to be a good person and have high ideals and do the right things. But this is where it gets a little tricky: doing those things which the Bible calls *good works* will never erase the wrongs (sins) we have committed. It's not about the good outweighing the bad; it's about Jesus clearing our sin right out of existence in the eyes of God. And this can be accomplished only by accepting God's gift of grace.

What Kind of Relationship Does God Want?

Well, **Hosea 6:6** tells us, *"I don't want your sacrifices — I want your love; I don't want your offerings — I want you to know me."* Clearly, this verse points out the relationship God wants with us; it should be mutual, and we shouldn't try to buy the relationship with sacrifices and offerings (self-imposed compensation for our sins to God). It should be a shared friendship.

Note: Some good works are acceptable to God if done out of gratitude for His gift of salvation or done in the spirit of humility when serving Him. God states that doing those types of good works will have eternal benefits.

Another Flaw in the Good Works Theory

What if we didn't have time to do any good works for God? How would we be saved? From the example of the criminal on the cross next to Jesus, we can see that doing good works has nothing to do with our salvation. This was made perfectly clear in Jesus' response to that criminal on the cross next to Him, which is recorded in the **Gospel of Luke 23:32–33:**

> *"Two other men, both criminals, were also led out with Him (Jesus) to be executed. When they came to the place called the Skull, they crucified Him there, along with the criminals—one on His right, the other on His left."*

Then we read in **Luke 23:39–43:**

> *"One of the criminals who hung there hurled insults at Him (Jesus): 'Aren't you the Messiah? Save yourself and us!' But the other criminal rebuked Him. 'Don't you fear God,' he said, 'since you are under the same sentence? We are punished justly, for we are getting what our deeds deserve. But this man has done nothing wrong.' Then he said, 'Jesus, remember me when you come into your Kingdom.' Jesus answered him, 'I*

tell you the truth, today you will be with me in paradise.'"

The criminal on the cross next to Jesus, when rebuking the criminal on the cross on the other side of Jesus, admitted that he and his fellow criminal were guilty of the crimes they had committed and were getting their just rewards. He also expressed to the other criminal, and everyone within earshot, that Jesus did nothing wrong: He was an innocent man unjustly condemned. When the criminal asked, "Don't you fear God?" he also assumed there was going to be some sort of judgement coming, and he didn't want to be part of it. With this, the criminal asks Jesus to remember him: *"Jesus, remember me when you come into your Kingdom."* Appreciating that only God has a Kingdom in the eternity, the criminal did three things that day: 1) He admitted he was guilty and worthy of penalty of the cross. 2) He acknowledged Jesus was innocent and God. 3) He asked for Jesus to remember him, even though he was unworthy of what he was asking.

The moment *"Jesus answered him, 'Truly I tell you, today you will be with me in paradise,'"* that criminal went from being Hell-bound to Heaven-bound. He didn't have time to go to church or confession or read the Scriptures, and he didn't have time to do any great acts of kindness or work in the soup kitchen. All he had time for was to believe by faith what Jesus had just said to him: *"Truly I tell you, today you will be with me in paradise."*

I can just imagine the scene at Heaven's gate a few hours later: "Hey, you (the criminal), what are you doing here?"

Answer: "The guy on the centre cross, Jesus, said I could come in."

That is why I am so glad the criminal's account of salvation is in the Bible, for it shows me that my former thinking (I have to do good works to earn my way to Heaven) was flawed and will not be factored in when I arrive at Heaven's gate. The only thing that will be factored in is my answer to the question *why are you here?* And I can reply with enthusiasm, "Jesus, the one who died on the cross—said I could come in."

Grace with No Strings Attached

It's like this: I have come upon hard times and squandered all of my money foolishly on get-rich-quick schemes. On top of that, I lost my job because I was late too many times. I have become delinquent on my mortgage, and the bank will not give me any more extensions; eviction is inevitable. I'm pleading with everyone I know to help me, but no one is able, or in reality, wants to.

A man hears of my predicament and goes to the bank on my behalf. He pays off all of the penalties and completely pays the mortgage. Now, my standing at the bank is restored. The man then comes to my family and me with the mortgage deed marked "paid in full". As he hands me the papers, all he asks in return is nothing more than a thank you. I owe nothing else. We stand at the door, stunned; then all at once, we run back into the house, rummaging through every room, looking for any money we can find. We come up with a handful of loose change and offer it to him.

The look on the generous man's face is one of utter disbelief. He says to me, "I have offered you your house back, paid in full, and you offer me in return a handful of coins. Have you no humility to accept my gift as it was intended? What will you say to those that asked what happened here today? Will you say that a good man helped me out of debt, omitting that your response was so insufficient that it's demeaning? You prideful man, I rescind my offer that you didn't deserve in the first place."

The illustration above shows how absurd it would be for the family to give the man a handful of change for a gift of that magnitude. When we die and stand before God, He will put a simple question to us: "Why should I let you into My Heaven?" If we present a list of the best of our lives—and that is exactly what the Bible says the multitudes will do—aren't we being just as absurd as the family offering a few coins to the generous man in return for his kindness? The family didn't deserve the generous man's kindness or compassion, just as we don't deserve God's generosity, compassion, or kindness offered through Jesus Christ. The only way to receive the gift of God's grace is to fully know in our hearts that we don't deserve it and humbly accept it by faith.

The Meaning of Grace

"Grace is an essential part of God's character. Grace is closely related to God's benevolence, love, and mercy. Grace can be variously defined as *God's favour toward the unworthy* or *God's benevolence on the undeserving*. In His grace, God is willing to forgive us and bless us abundantly, in spite of the fact that we don't deserve to be treated so well or dealt with so generously (gotquestions.org)."[v]

To receive grace or any undeserved gift is hard, for we are not wired that way. I once had a man offer me a tip after he paid me for repairing his car. For a car mechanic, that is an unusual occurrence. I didn't know how to act, plus the amount of money offered was way too much. I ended up handling it all wrong, embarrassing him and myself. The hurt on the man's face was evident. The gift was a lot of money to me, but to him, it wasn't very much because of our different stations in life. In the end, I took the money, but I took away his joy in giving it. In this instance, I thought I was doing the right thing by making a fuss about accepting it, but really it was just my pride getting in the way. Over the years, I have found that my pride has gotten in the way of so many good things that were offered to me.

What I learned through this is that if someone offers me something, I just accept the gift as intended with humility and joy. The outcome is, the giver feels the joy of giving, and I, the recipient, also feel joy and benefit from the gift.

Can you see the similarities to how God might feel when He offers His free gift of salvation, and our response is to try to add our own good works. It takes away God's joy in offering us the greatest gift ever presented: a gift of inconceivable price and value, a gift given out of total love—the gift of His Son.

As I pointed out before, any justification that you think is coming from keeping the Ten Commandments is not forthcoming. Those who think that way show a lack of understanding about God's grace and the separation that has been created between God and man because of sin.

As long as there is self-justification, the one who is justifying will never see a need for God's gift of grace. That is why those who come to God must humble themselves. For if Christ humbled Himself by becoming obedient to death—even death on a cross—for our sake, shouldn't we follow His example of humility when coming to God for the precious gift of salvation?

> *"Humble yourselves before the Lord, and He will lift you up."* – **James 4:10**

Head Knowledge Versus Heart Knowledge

You may believe in God. You may go to church, pray before you eat, and even give to God's work. These are all good things to do. But if you don't comprehend the difference between merely believing with your head in God's existence as opposed to believing with your heart, that's a problem. Even the fallen angels that are called demons know the difference. **James 2:19** says, *"You believe that there is one God. Good! Even the demons believe that and tremble."*

Where did these demons come from? Well, when a third of the angels in Heaven sinned, at that moment they became demons and were cast out of God's presence. They know firsthand the power and glory of God. The demons even interacted with Christ when He was on earth. They know the coming judgement and are doing everything in their power to keep mankind under that same judgement. But, as we have read, page after page, God does not want to keep us under judgement; instead, He wants to redeem us for Himself. For the demons, no redemption will ever be given. So, just having head knowledge of God simply puts you in the same class as fallen angels. Only believing with your heart, by faith in God's saving grace (Jesus), is going to achieve reconciliation with Him.

I have known quite a few people over the years who are in the situation described above: they have lots of knowledge about God and can even quote Scripture from the Bible. But other than on Sunday morning, their lives don't resemble the fact that they even know God. Living out **Matthew 15:8,** *"These people honour me with their lips, but their hearts are far from me."* I often wonder what it's going to take for them to embrace **Romans 10:9:** *"If you declare with your mouth, 'Jesus is Lord' and believe in your heart that God raised Him from the dead, you will be saved."*

Initially, I had a little of what I call 'head knowledge'. Even though I had never read the Bible, if anyone had asked me about God, I would parrot what I had heard at one time or another. The hearsay statement I would use was, "I am a good person, and that will get me into Heaven."

That's why it took me so long to realize that I needed a Saviour. I was trusting in my own so-called 'goodness' that was derived by "keeping" the Ten Commandments. Keep in mind that my understanding of the Ten Commandments' redeeming powers was used as a yardstick measurement to find others who measured up shorter than me. Figuring that as long as I was above anyone, anyone at all, in my mind, I was okay. With this view, I didn't think I was lost. Looking back, that was some very foolish thinking.

If you don't know you're lost, you're not looking to be found.

When did I realize I was a sinner? When I started to see my sin as God views it. Stretching the truth is dishonest—lying; looking at the opposite sex in the wrong way—adultery; not fulfilling promises—disobedience; building myself up— egotistical; grumpy and unkind—anger; talking behind someone's back—malice. Finally, seeing these sins and many others in my life for what they really were in God's eyes— unacceptable—it became evident that I was lost.

Agreeing with what the Bible says concerning sin, I was going to be condemned to Hell. It didn't matter what I believed condemning sin was; I had to go by what God said it is. The few verses I have already quoted from the Bible state clearly what sin is and what punishment awaits the unforgiven sinner.

That's when I figured it out: no one, including me, was ever going to be good enough to go to Heaven without a Saviour. Thankfully, God provided a Saviour in the person of Jesus Christ.

You might wonder which of my sins was so terrible that it convinced me that I was Hell-bound and not Heaven-bound. It wasn't one specific sin, but my realization that my attitude towards sin was way off base. My personal convictions didn't line up with the Bible in so many areas. When the Holy Spirit opened my eyes to see my sin from God's perspective, that's when I really started to take a good look at my life because I wanted my final destination to be Heaven—not Hell.

Conviction of Sin

At times, in quiet moments of reflection, I just felt lost, broken, and unloved. I thought about how easily I had put someone down to build myself up, without even giving a second thought as to how I made that person feel. I remembered how I had worked hard to be recognized and then ensured that everyone heard how great I was because of it. I could not erase the fact that these were the actions of a man filled with arrogance and pride, both of which God despises. And I realized that both traits dominated all parts of my life and were manifested in my expression of harshness and anger at others around me. I didn't want to be that guy, but the problem was that, in any situation, I could become "that guy" in a split second by demonstrating inconsiderate and harsh behaviour.

God was showing me that I was never going to win the battle of pride in my life in my own humanity—I needed Him. That's when I found out that receiving Christ was not just about being spared from going to Hell; it was a relationship that would change the believer from the inside out over time. It would be nice if the new believer was completely made perfect on the day of conversion, but conforming to the will of God and the image of Christ is a growing process over a lifetime.

What does it mean to conform to the will of God? It's complying with His rules and standards for living. **1 Peter 2:3** says, *"Like newborn babies, crave pure spiritual milk, so that by* *it you may grow up in your salvation, now that you have tasted that the Lord is good."*

From the time we are born, we are taught how to live in the context of a family, with the goal of growing into maturity. It's the same for the new believer learning to be part of God's family. We have to learn how to act and grow into maturity in the context of being a child of God.

The best way to learn to be part of God's family is to imitate the one that made no mistakes, Jesus Christ. To help with this, God pairs new believers with mature believers in Christ, so they can see firsthand how to walk and grow in Christ on a daily basis.

It's kind of like when I started my apprenticeship to be a mechanic: I was paired up with a veteran mechanic, and I would mimic him, learning to do the repairs that he did with ease. At first, for me, they were hard; but after time and practice, I became the veteran mechanic and did those same repairs with ease. Over time, I too, built a foundation of knowledge that equipped me to work on my own, though still under the veteran mechanic's watchful eye. He did own the place.

Years down the road, when I had become the veteran mechanic, I was able to train younger apprentices on how to be good, solid technicians. Whether it's learning to be a mechanic or learning to be more like Christ, or just learning life principles in general, learning from those who have mastered the trade is always worthwhile. For our goal should always be to become mature believers in Christ, so that we too can be used by God to accomplish His will—to His Glory.

Over the years in my spiritual life, I have built a foundation of knowledge drawn from the Bible of who Jesus is and how to emulate Him, growing into His image. But I never work on my own; I constantly rely on the Holy Spirit to teach me. I also am thankful for the men of God who, by their personal walk with Christ, give me good examples of how to grow. As I said, becoming more like Christ is a lifelong adventure.

Hopefully, reading through this chapter, God's grace is understood as a gift that we don't deserve, can't work for, and is only offered to us because of His benevolent and merciful love towards us. The next chapter puts a value on God's grace by giving some understanding on what it took to save us from judgement and Hell.

The next chapter also deals with the reality of Hell, judgement, and society's views on those subjects. For if we know the peril of what we are being saved from, it will be motivation to live our lives for God wholeheartedly.

7

JUDGEMENT AND HELL

A Reality We Have to Deal With

Refusing to believe in a coming judgement and a place called Hell doesn't void its validity. C. S. Lewis once wrote, concerning Hell, "There is no doctrine which I would more willingly remove from Christianity than this, if it lay in my power. But it has the full support of Scripture and, specially, of our Lord's own words; it has always been held by Christendom; and it has the support of reason."[vi]

As much as C. S. Lewis would like to remove Hell, he said: "It's not in our power to disregard the teaching of Hell in the Bible."[vii]

In fact, the thought of people spending eternity in Hell for rejecting God's offer of salvation is heartbreaking. Hell is a difficult truth, but it is something about which Jesus spoke more than anyone else in Scripture. Jesus didn't talk about Hell as an abstract idea, but rather, as a real, physical place, just as He did with Heaven.

Even though Jesus was the one describing Hell, many disregard His teaching on the subject. And why wouldn't they? No one wants to think about a place of eternal judgement. In my finite human existence, I have a hard time reconciling in my mind the concept that space has no ending and that we are going to live on forever, so trying to comprehend anyone actually living in Hell for eternity is difficult. Especially when this could include my family and friends whom I love and cherish. But Jesus told us what will happen to those who will not accept His offer of salvation.

I also don't believe that we can treasure the description of Heaven, and at the same time disregard the description of Hell because it's an uncomfortable thought. We may hope that if we don't even address Hell at all, it may just vanish. And from what I have read, the belief in a real Hell has vanished in many churches and in most people's line of thinking. But to believe in what Jesus has to say about Heaven, and I mean really believe, I have to take Him at His word: that Heaven exists and that its magnificence is beyond comprehension. But can I truly believe that statement, and then totally disregard His teachings and warnings about Hell? Well, let's see if I can answer that question in the following paragraphs.

Can we take Jesus' word that Hell is a real, physical place?

Let's Look at It This Way

If a good friend of mine visited the Venezuelan jungles, came across some lost ruins, and was unable to take any pictures of his discovery because the high humidity would wreck his camera, do I disregard his description of the ruins due to his lack of physical proof? Or do I take him at his word because I know that his character is above reproach and that his honesty is a part of who he is? **Yes,** I would take him at his word, for I would have no reason not to. But when it comes down to Jesus, who is incapable of lying, giving us a description of Hell, that seems to be a very different story for most people.

We all know people who, when they tell a story, we have to take everything they say with a 'grain of salt', meaning you have to pick out the truth from the exaggerations. Do you think Jesus should be lumped in the same category as the 'grain of salt' guy? No, I wouldn't think so, but by dismissing what Jesus says about Hell, that is exactly what is taking place.

For me, I can't overlook the fact that there are over 162 references in the New Testament that warn us about Hell. Over 70 of these references were uttered by the Lord Jesus Himself. Jesus' authority when it comes to Heaven and Hell is established in the fact that He was the creator of both. In the light of Him being the creator of Heaven and Hell, by not believing in their existence, you are basically calling Jesus a liar.

Let's put it in this context: if you told me something that only happened to you and my response was, "I can't believe that," the first thing out of your mouth would probably be, "Are you calling me a liar?" So, you can see the similarity when we dismiss any part of God's Word: God assumes He is being called a liar. That is the normal response anyone would have if not believed when telling the truth.

"Oh, come on, Mike: the Bible is just a book of stories; no one takes it literally." I hope for your sake that you are right—but, if you're not and the Bible is God's infallible Word, the information already established up to this point in the book should be enough for you to realize that, without Christ, the instant you stand before God will be your worst moment that will continue for eternity. That, my friend, is a major gamble, and one I wouldn't want to see you make.

Since Jesus was very straightforward when talking about the consequences of Hell, diminishing Hell's significance would really be an attack on His integrity. If Jesus' words lose integrity, everything He says becomes irrelevant or powerless to make a difference in anyone's life. To have full confidence in Jesus' words—their authenticity must stand on who Jesus is—God.

Jesus describes Hell in **Matthew 8:12** as, *"total separation, darkness, and a place of weeping and gnashing of teeth."* So, how do those in today's society react to Jesus' description of Hell?

Well, some don't believe there is a real Hell—and they refuse to be persuaded otherwise. Others say Hell is in the Bible to frighten people into believing and obedience. There are also those that say Hell is just a myth, entertaining like many other stories in the Bible, but certainly nothing anyone should be foolish enough to take literally. Finally, there are those like me who believe Hell is a literal place, and to be avoided at all costs.

My understanding through discussions on the topic of Hell is that my belief in a literal Hell is not widely accepted. Those who don't want to accept or even acknowledge the Hell of the Bible, but still wish to use the Bible as a basis for faith, have a real conundrum. How can this conundrum be resolved? The Apostle Paul gives an explanation in **2 Timothy 4:3:** *"For a time is coming when people will no longer listen to sound and wholesome teaching. They will follow their own desires and will look for teachers who will tell them whatever their itching ears want to hear."*

While it's that simple, if you don't want to be bothered by the doctrine of Hell, then just blindly align yourself with teachers that tell you what you want to hear: teachers who say that they are of God, presenting a non-confrontational doctrine, which is easy to believe, using only positive non-judgmental words—creating a feel-good religion that's for everybody. The big problem is that this religion is devoid of God; it contains very little truth and leads many people unknowingly to Hell. How can this happen? The simple reason is that today's society, as a whole, doesn't want to seek out any verification for what is being taught in God's name, nor do they believe the Bible is a book of absolute truth.

I can perceive the question in your head on that statement: where is the hard evidence that validates the Bible as absolute truth? Good question. The chapters in this book on Bible interpretation and prophecies leave little doubt in the discerning mind that the Bible is unquestionably the Word of God. In addition, archaeological finds prove that the Bible has another aspect—it is, in fact, one of the greatest history books ever written.

The next question is, why is it so hard to believe in solid Biblical truths? Because it's easier to believe in the statement, which I have heard many times, "As long as you believe in something, you're okay, for God is love." Basically, that statement takes away all of our responsibilities to follow God as He prescribes, eliminating the God that judges humanity. It also takes Hell out of the picture and any other uncomfortable scenario that comes with following a righteous God. This line of thinking disregards all of the Biblical teachings on condemnation of sin, coming judgement, and Hell; it dilutes Biblical doctrine, deteriorating the very foundation on which a strong faith is built and leaving in its wake a feel-good faith of no substance or value that is easily influenced by, as written in **2 Timothy 2:3,** *"teachers who will tell them whatever their itching ears want to hear,"* which aligns with "The New Reality".

What happens when a society just can't comprehend the reality of a physical place called Hell? Well, today's society is in the process of making up a new reality: one without a Biblical Hell.

The big problem with that is that no one can make up a new reality, for the word reality means *the state of things as they actually exist.* Since Hell really exists, this new "reality" is nothing more than lies.

Here is the doctrine of **The New Reality:** it still accepts Jesus, but denies His godship and His blood atonement for sin. In the process, it denies judgement, punishment, and Hell. In essence, **The New Reality** has redefined what sin is and how we look at it by denying that absolute truth exists and shifting the authority of the Bible to man.

A coherent standard of rules for all to follow is crucial to the survival of any society. That standard gives us the authority to administer justice and creates a guideline for what is socially acceptable. In the past, that standard came from the Bible; but today it seems to be moving in the direction of peoples' personal feelings, wants, and desires.

This new standard is originating from the belief that "if something feels true to you, it's truth; if it feels right to you, it's right; and if it feels real to you, it's your reality." It's okay to have your own thoughts and feelings, but when a certain group believes or groups believe that their thoughts and feelings should be implemented as the standard for all of society, that's a problem. Which group do we follow? Which group should have dominance? Where does the standard of truth come from? What about God's standard of truth? Does it now become irrelevant? Or do we just pick and choose which of God's standards of behaviour fits into our new reality and then disregard the rest?

This will ultimately be seen as freedom at first—breaking free from what some see as God's suffocating rules to live by— but in the end, **Proverbs 14:12** will become the 'reality': *"Before every man there lies a wide and pleasant road that seems right but ends in (spiritual) death."*

But this New Reality of reducing Jesus to a mere man, redefining sin, denying judgement, punishment, and Hell is taking off. I am not making it up. It is obvious, though, that it's not enhancing our society. If you take a good look at how this society is doing during the process of removing absolute truth, you see the results are confusion and turmoil on a worldwide scale.

Note that I am referring to "absolute truth" in this setting as God's Word. Remember, God's Word as found in the Bible is true at all times, never outdated in any circumstance, and will never change.

This isn't the first society to substitute something else for God. Just explore the Roman Empire or any other empire in the history books. Without absolute truth, failure of a society is inevitable.

You have the choice to believe in whatever you want. God gives you absolute freedom to choose, but be aware—there are consequences for the choices we make. You can reject the concept of a real Hell and embrace **The New Reality**, or anything else for that matter. It's totally up to you. Unfortunately, Hell is part of God's absolute truth, as is Heaven, and no matter what you want to believe, nothing is going to change that. The consequences of embracing **The New Reality** is that you are probably going to end up in a Hell you don't believe exists.

The Bible teaches us that God made Hell, plain and simple. We may not agree with it. We may even resolve in our hearts to never follow a God who would create such a place of suffering for those who don't believe, as the Bible specifies. And that's okay, you have the free will to make that choice. But being mad at God when He endured such a great suffering on our behalf to give us an alternative to Hell seems a little short-sighted. For the reality of the situation is that God didn't reject us but is reaching out to us. If we reject Him and His offer of grace, we condemn our own souls to Hell.

Hell is probably going to be far worse than what we can imagine, for it is described as a total separation and abandonment from everyone. The only way to avoid Hell is by getting to know God's love, which is pure and poured out towards us by His grace. Once you come to understand His righteousness, perfect judgements, and compassion for all mankind, it doesn't take long to get excited about learning more about Him; then we find that He is a gracious and just God, and that His grace towards us is unmerited, but freely given to all who would ask.

After you have determined these things to be true, try to persuade as many as you can to trust in Him as well so that all can avoid the consequence of Hell. Then take solace in the fact that one day, we will see Him in person, and on that day, all things will be revealed to us, and we will understand the Master's plan completely. On that day, when all is revealed, you don't want to be standing on the wrong side of the fence saying to yourself, "Oh, shoot, I didn't get that one right. Oops." Eternity is forever.

You may feel that I am overemphasizing Hell, but it is very significant to the Christian faith and needs to be understood. The Bible actually gives very few particulars about Hell, but we do know that it was originally intended for demonic spiritual beings, and not people **(Matthew 25:41).** The experience of being in Hell is compared to burning **(Mark 9:43; 9:48; Matthew 18:9; Luke 16:24).** At the same time, Hell is compared to darkness **(Matthew 22:13)** and associated with intense grief **(Matthew 8:12)** and horror **(Mark 9:44).**

"In short, the Bible tells us only what being in Hell is like; it does not explicitly say what Hell is or exactly how it functions. What the Bible does make clear is that Hell is real, eternal, and **to be avoided at all costs (Matthew 5:29–30).** [gotquestions.org]"[viii]

All Scripture mentioned above contains the words of Jesus—the same Jesus who talks about Heaven also spoke about Hell because He wanted us to see what He was going to endure on the cross on our behalf. If Hell doesn't exist, the question that has to be answered is, "Why would Jesus allow Himself to suffer on the cross?"

"I do not set aside the grace of God, for if righteousness could be gained through the law, Christ died for nothing." **(Galatians 3:21)**

The fact that it is beyond my ability—and the ability of most of humanity—to comprehend Hell doesn't change anything. What I do know, is that, when the Bible is watered down to fit our own rationalization of Scripture we don't understand, truth dies. Without truth, we are susceptible to all kinds of deception because the standard of what is right is lost. Since God is truth, we also lose Him by picking and choosing what parts of His Word we regard as authentic. For it's as simple as this: we must be willing to accept all of God's Word to have total confidence in any of God's Word.

If you just can't accept the concept of Hell, I understand; I wish I didn't have too, either. But I can't take the chance of changing one letter of the Word of God. For modifying any of the Word of God that doesn't suit me would certainly lead to further falsification of Scripture to fit any contradictory lifestyle choices. This ultimately opens the door to being, as **Ephesians 4:14** says, *"Blown here and there by every wind of teaching and by the cunning and craftiness of people in their deceitful scheming."* There is only one way to defend against being consumed by the deceptions of false teachers, and that is having a foundation of faith that comes from accurately knowing God's Holy Scripture in its entirety, as written.

Every believer and non-believer will be judged by the Word of God. When judged, every one of us will be stripped of our persona of who they think they are and stand before God totally vulnerable and exposed. As described in **Hebrews 4:12–13,** *"For the word of God is alive and active. Sharper than any double-edged sword, it penetrates even to dividing soul and spirit, joints and marrow; it judges the thoughts and attitudes of the heart. Nothing in all creation is hidden from God's sight. Everything is uncovered and laid bare before the eyes of him to whom we must give account."* The only difference in the believer who stands before God is that no eternal judgement or punishment will be given. These are some sobering thoughts for both the believer and the non-believer.

Is there a chance that you feel in your heart that there is truth in what was written in **Hebrews 4:12–13**? Well, the same truth was spoken by Jesus in **Matthew 12:36–37:** *"But I tell you that everyone will have to give account on the day of judgment for every empty word they have spoken. For by your words you* *will be acquitted, and by your words you will be condemned."* If you are not sure how you will make out on the day of judgement when you have to give an account for every word ever spoken or thought, and every deed you have ever done, then maybe it's time to consider asking God for help. He promises if you seek Him with all your heart, you will find Him: *"You will seek me and find me when you seek me with all you heart"* **(Jeremiah 29:13).**

Asking God for help is not hard: just bow your head and pray for your eyes to be opened to see the truths in Scripture by the power of the Holy Spirit. If it is truly the desire of your heart, God promises to open your eyes to the answers. When I prayed from my heart to God for answers, that is exactly what I received. I didn't necessarily get the answers I was expecting, but I received the answers I needed to bring peace into my life. The answers I received changed my life, which I have never regretted.

On Judgement Day, No Excuses Will Be Valid

I hope it's clear by now that everyone will have to give an account to God—the One who sees all—for their time spent here on earth. Are you starting to believe what the Bible says about sin, Heaven and Hell? Or do you still choose to believe that the Bible is just a book of interesting stories and a guide for living if we choose it, that it has no real power to change lives, and there is no judgement or punishment for our actions? If this is what you believe, and you're not going to be persuaded otherwise, you might wonder why you should continue reading. **I can think of one really good reason:** if what is written here has any merit at all, you may already be condemned, and if I were a condemned man, I would certainly do everything in my power to find out if there were any options for being pardoned.

Please don't stake where you spend eternity on the overused statement: "God is love and all will be forgiven." As I said before, this statement is not corroborated in the Bible by any means; but many are staking where they will spend eternity on that statement alone.

Again, why read on? Because, if you do, you may come to the conclusion that there is truth in what you are reading. And that truth is that God wants a relationship with you. A truth like that, if acted upon, will change your life for eternity. Or if you finish the book and still don't want to believe what is written, you will have read some interesting stories and maybe will have learned a few things from the Bible.

The following pages explain how sin entered the world, explain more about Heaven and Hell, and explain why Christ's Deity is so important to the fulfillment of the Good News of the Gospels—forgiveness of sin. It's prudent to accept nothing based on assumptions, but to follow through to discern for yourself the authenticity of Biblical truth, making that truth the basis of your faith. Don't operate based on unsubstantiated hearsay, as I did for many years; that kept me in darkness. Eternity is forever, and you will have no second chance to change your mind after you draw that last breath. *"Just as people are destined to die once, and after that to face judgement"* **(Hebrews 9:27).**

It's so obvious that sin is not healthy for our eternal souls, so where did it start?

8

THE FALL OF MANKIND

The Prelude to the Fall

The fall in the Garden, written out below, was masterminded by a very crafty serpent. Where did this serpent come from? The serpent was a fallen angel called Satan, and he was originally from Heaven, until he sinned and was thrown out.

Satan's Sin

God created the angels as ministering servants—divided into three groups: one-third under Lucifer, one-third under Gabriel, and one-third under Michael.

One-third of those angels sinned; Lucifer and his angels rebelled against God. Lucifer said, *"I will exalt myself. I will be like the Most High. I will ascend into the heavens."* Lucifer's prideful statements were sin against God. God had already determined the payment for sin, and Satan and his followers were condemned to that place called Hell. Satan and his angels (now called demons), were cast out of Heaven and are awaiting their final destination—Hell.

The Deception in the Garden of Eden

"Now the serpent was more crafty than any of the wild animals the Lord God had made. He said to the woman, 'Did God really say, "You must not eat from any tree in the garden?"' The woman said to the serpent, 'We may eat fruit from the trees in the garden, but God did say, "You must not eat fruit from the tree that is in the middle of the garden, and you must not touch it, or you will die."' 'You will not certainly die,' the serpent said to the woman. 'For God knows that when you eat from it your eyes will be opened, and you will be like God, knowing good and evil.' When the woman saw that the fruit of the tree was good for food and pleasing to the eye, and also desirable for gaining wisdom, she took some and ate it. She also gave some to her husband, who was with her, and he ate it. Then the eyes of both of them were opened, and they realized they were naked; so they sewed fig leaves together and made coverings for themselves. Then the man and his wife heard the sound of the Lord God as he was walking in the garden in the cool of the day, and they hid from the Lord God among the trees of the

garden. But the Lord God called to the man, 'Where are you?' He answered, 'I heard you in the garden, and I was afraid because I was naked; so I hid.' And he said, 'Who told you that you were naked? Have you eaten from the tree that I commanded you not to eat from?' The man said, 'The woman you put here with me—she gave me some fruit from the tree, and I ate it.' Then the Lord God said to the woman, 'What is this you have done?' The woman said, 'The serpent deceived me, and I ate.'" – **Genesis 3:3–13**

Through Adam and Eve's disobedience, sin entered the world. They had no excuse for their actions as they had been clearly warned and told what not to do; they were told that any act of disobedience would result in death. The consequences for disobeying God were predetermined before man was ever created: God had told the angels, who also had free will, that Hell had been created for any who disobeyed His Word.

The Bible tells us Hell is a place of conscience and memory where people remember opportunities in life to avoid Hell.

Not one single man was alive when God made Hell. God didn't make Hell for man; He made Hell as a place of punishment for any who sinned. When Satan and the angels under his care turned away from God, that was the first act of sin.

When Adam ate the forbidden fruit, sin entered the world, and everyone who has been born since has been born a sinner. This makes all of humanity, from start to finish, sinful and guilty before God. Mankind finds itself in the same predicament as

Satan and his angels: condemned and awaiting punishment. This statement is substantiated by **Romans 5:12:** *"Therefore just as sin entered the world through one man and death through sin, and in this way death came to all men."*

Satan seduced man as told in **Genesis 3:4–5:** *" 'You will not certainly die,' the serpent (Satan) said to the woman. 'For God knows that when you eat from it your eyes will be opened, and you will be like God, knowing good and evil.' "*

Mankind disobeyed God, refusing to listen to His warnings; they went their own way, and, unfortunately for us, we inherited their sinfulness and the predetermined punishment for their act of rebellion.

Basically, man became proud and committed the same sin as Satan: "I'll decide what's right and wrong. I'll run my own life. I'll sit on the throne of my heart. I'll make my own decisions. I'll do what I want to do. I'll go where I want to go. I'll be what I want to be."

If the outcome of eating from the Tree of the Knowledge of Good and Evil was going to be so devastating to mankind, why was that tree even put in the Garden of Eden in the first place? Because without choice, do we really have free will? Without choice, can we truly love and be loved? God gave us free will to be able to choose to love and follow Him; for without free will, we can do neither of those willingly. The outcome of Adam and Eve eating from the Tree of the Knowledge of Good and Evil would remain absolutely devastating if God, by His love for us, didn't give us a choice to be reconciled to Him through Jesus

Christ. Jesus is the only one not born of sin since Adam and Eve ate from the tree they were commanded to avoid.

We can't see the whole picture at this point, but God does; and for God to let His Son be sacrificed for our behalf, the end result must be magnificence.

The Bible's Hard Truth about the Condemnation of Mankind

Simply put, we are born into sin, and no sin can enter Heaven. Once you are born, you are headed for Hell unless you believe in Christ. This is verified by **John 3:18,** which says, *"Whoever believes in Him is not condemned, but whoever does not believe stands condemned already because they have not believed in the name of God's one and only Son."*

I wasn't taught that way growing up. My understanding was that we were all going to Heaven, but if you did enough bad things, the scales would tip, and you would end up in Hell. That is a fallacy; it's not the amount of sin we do. It's that we were born with a sinful nature resulting from the fall in the Garden of Eden. The choice to go to Hell is not ours. It's the default. But the good news is that the choice to go to Heaven instead of Hell *is* ours.

God loves us and doesn't want to see any of us perish. What does it mean to perish? Well, the dictionary defines it like this: "to suffer complete ruin or destruction." [ix] God defines perish as total separation from Him for eternity, in a place called Hell.

The Bible tells us in **2 Peter 3:9,** *"The Lord is not slow in keeping his promise, as some understand slowness. Instead he is patient with you, not wanting anyone to perish, but everyone to come to repentance."* In essence, God doesn't want to see anyone go to Hell.

So, what's the problem? Why doesn't God just let everyone into Heaven? The problem is that God can't go back on His Word. *"God is not man, that he should lie, or a son of man, that he should change his mind. Has he said, and will he not do it? Or has he spoken, and will he not fulfill it?"* **(Numbers 23:19).** And since God's Word says no sinful person can enter Heaven, God needed to find a way to make the sinful righteous.

When Adam stepped into the trap of sin, he took all mankind with him. Since then, all of mankind is in a trap that wasn't made for us—resulting in a severed relationship with God. But God, wanting to restore His relationship with mankind, made a way out of the trap that holds us captive. God did this by using the sacrificial death of Jesus on the cross as payment for all who wanted to be released and have a restored relationship with Him. God did this without changing His nature. Though angels are offered no escape, God made a way out of the trap for man.

I know what you are thinking: *who, when caught in a trap, wouldn't want to be released?* This trap of sin is disguised to its captives as freedom, with all the pleasures one could desire; this trap offers the illusion of choice to do and be anything we desire. It doesn't appear to be a bad place.

It's not until death occurs and we stand before God that the harsh reality of the trap of sin is revealed. Standing before the judgement seat of God without excuse, the payment of man's soul is required. What's sad is that most people refuse to open their eyes to the conviction of the Holy Spirit to see their dilemma until it's too late.

The Conclusion Regarding How God Sees Sin

I've talked a lot about sin: what it is, how mankind is saturated with it, and how it has separated us from fellowship with God. Once again, if we don't understand that we are sinners, this puts us in a dire situation with God. Without this understanding, we will not see our need for a Saviour and come to Christ. If we don't try to see our sinful nature as God views it, we may try other paths to find God: exploring other religions, thinking up foolish ideas about who God is, becoming confused, and ultimately, trying to justify ourselves. Unfortunately, the outcome will always be the same when we don't follow God's plan—we will end up condemned to Hell for eternity.

When we don't see our sinfulness, we can come up with some very foolish ideas; such as thinking we don't need a Saviour. That can even seem right to us. But God says differently in **Proverbs 14:12:** *"There is a way which seems right to a man, but its end is the way of death."*

Another popular, foolish idea is that we are able to fabricate our own righteousness by righteous acts. God has a different view on that too. *"All of us have become like one who is unclean, and all our righteous acts are like filthy rags; we all shrivel up like a leaf, and like the wind our sins sweep us away"* **(Isaiah 64:6).**

What it comes down to is that man is either washed clean by the blood of Christ or he is not. It's the difference between being clean or unclean. That which is clean or pure is in its proper place, whereas that which is unclean or impure is disgustingly out of place.

The Bible tells us that our good works outside of Christ are unclean like filthy rags. Without receiving Christ's gift of forgiveness, we are just disgustingly out of place in God's view.

But the good news is that through Christ's work on the cross, we are cleansed from all unrighteousness, going from being disgustingly out of place in God's eyes to becoming pure and in proper standing with Him.

I think that if we believe what the Bible says—that we are all sinners—we can also believe the same Bible when it talks about the gift of God's grace. *"For it is by grace you have been saved, though faith—and this not from yourselves, it is the gift of God—not by works, so that no one can boast"* **(Ephesians 2:8).** Many of the verses quoted make it very evident that our faith is very important to God and placing our faith in Jesus Christ (God's gift to us) is the only way a relationship with God can be restored.

Billy Graham preached, "However, remember that whether our sins are relatively small or great, they will place us in Hell apart from God's grace. **The good news is** that Jesus paid the penalty for our sins and the sins of the whole world on the cross. If we will repent and turn to Jesus by faith, our sins will be forgiven, and we will receive the **gift of eternal life**."[x]

What does Billy Graham mean by "repent?" The dictionary defines it as "to feel or express sincere regret or remorse about one's wrongdoing or sin."[xi] The Bible goes further: not only do we feel remorse about our sin, but we turn from our sin and go in another direction…God's direction.

Billy Graham gives us great encouragement as he sums up his walk with God. "My home is in Heaven. I'm just traveling through this world. Being a Christian is more than just an instantaneous conversion; it is a daily process whereby you grow to be more and more like Christ. A lifetime endeavour."[xii]

9

JESUS CHRIST AND DEITY

If the object is to become more and more like Christ in this life, then we need to know who the Bible says He is. In **John 1:1–5,** He is called the Word. *"In the beginning was the Word (Christ), and the Word was with God, and the Word was God. He was with God in the beginning. Through Him (Christ) all things were made that has been made. (all creation). In him was life, and that life was the light of all mankind. The light shines in the darkness, and the darkness has not overcome it."*

From those verses alone, we learn that Jesus Christ was, in the beginning, called the **Word**; and that He, Himself, was God. Through the **Word,** all things that were made were made by Him (Jesus Christ). When Jesus was born, He went from being called the **Word** to being called **Jesus Christ.** He did not lose His **Deity** when becoming a man. **He was the perfect God/Man.**

"For in Christ all the fullness of the Deity lives in bodily form, and in Christ you have been brought to fullness. He is the head over every power and authority." – **Colossians 2:9–10**

What Is Biblical Deity?

Deity is God. Not *a* god, but *the* eternal God, who has no beginning or end, who is all powerful, who is Holy, above reproach, and able to step out of natural laws, not bound by anything. He is worthy of our worship, allegiance, friendship, and above all, our reverence.

So, Jesus Christ is that "God in the flesh." When becoming a man, He kept His Deity (Godhood). Why was keeping His Deity so important? Because it was imperative that He is who He said He was for His sacrifice on the cross to have any significance at all. (We will learn more about that later).

The Name of the True God: "I AM"

God the Father and Jesus use the same name to show their Deity, and the name they call themselves is **"I AM."** The first time we see this name used occurs in **Exodus 3:14** when God was recruiting Moses in the wilderness of Horeb, the mountain of God at the time. Moses was conversing with God about the misery of God's people in Egypt. God said to Moses that indeed He had seen the misery of His people in Egypt and was going to send Moses to Pharaoh so that he could lead the Israelites out of the land of Egypt to a better land, which would become the Promised Land. Moses protested, but God said He would be with Moses. Then Moses asked God how he should reply if people asked who sent him. In **Exodus 3:13–14,** God tells Moses what to say, revealing **God's Deity.** *"Moses said to God, 'Suppose I go to the Israelites and say to them, "The God of your fathers has sent me to you," and they ask me, "What is his name?" Then what shall I tell them?' God said to Moses, 'I AM who I AM. This is what you are to say to the Israelites: I AM has sent me to you.'"*

"I AM WHO I AM" or **"I AM the One who is"** emphasizes God's dynamic and active self-existence.

The Israelites would know exactly who Moses was referring to when he used the name **"I AM"** because it plainly states **God's total Deity.**

In the Gospel of **John 8:58,** when Jesus was speaking to the religious leaders at the temple, He used this very name, **"I AM,"** to describe Himself. *"'Very truly I tell you,' Jesus answered, 'before Abraham was born, I AM!'"*

As soon as He used the name **"I AM,"** the priests knew exactly what Jesus was saying. He was saying He was God, not a god, but **God with full Deity.** The religious leaders were blinded to who Jesus was because of their pride and the self-importance they put on themselves. When they heard Jesus using the name **"I AM,"** they picked up rocks to stone Him to death. Their concept of what God was going to look like when He came to earth "to fulfill the Old Testament prophesies" was totally wrong. They thought He would start with them and that they would be the centre of God's plans. I guess they were, but not in a good way.

Christ used the name **"I AM"** once again in **Revelation 1:8** when Christ said, "**'I AM'** the Alpha and the Omega says the Lord God, who is, and who was, and who is to come, The Almighty.'"

Alpha and Omega signifies the beginning and the end— nothing before and nothing after.

Jesus Christ Pictured in His Full Deity

The Apostle John says in **Revelation 1:12–18**:

"I turned around to see the voice that was speaking to me. And when I turned I saw seven golden lampstands, and among the lampstands was someone like a son of man, dressed in a robe reaching down to his feet and with a golden sash around his chest. The hair on his head was white like wool, as white as snow, and his eyes were like blazing fire. His feet were like bronze glowing in a furnace, and his voice was like the sound of rushing waters. In his right hand he held seven stars, and coming out of his mouth was a sharp, double-edged sword. His face was like the sun shining in all its brilliance. When I saw him, I fell at his feet as though dead. Then he (Christ) placed his right hand on me and said: 'Do not be afraid. I AM the First and the Last. I AM the Living One; I was dead, and now look, I AM alive for ever and ever! And I hold the keys of death and Hades.'"

Wow, what a picture! But this is still the Christ Jesus who wants a relationship with every man, woman, and child on this earth. This is also the same Jesus who loves us more than His own life. But this is also the Jesus that is coming back to set up His kingdom here on earth—not as a lowly carpenter, but as God in all His Power and Deity.

10

THE TRINITY
The Father, Son, and Holy Spirit

God the Father

We read in **Ephesians 1:3,** *"Praise be to the God and Father of our Lord Jesus Christ, who has blessed us in the heavenly realms with every spiritual blessing in Christ."* Jesus said in **John 10:29,** *"I and the Father are one."*

God gives those who accept Christ the Holy Spirit. Romans 5:5 says:

> *"And hope does not put us to shame, because God's love has been poured out into our hearts through the Holy Spirit, who has been given to us."*

The Holy Spirit: The Messenger of the Father

John 14:26 tells us:

"But the Advocate, the Holy Spirit, whom the Father will send in my name (Jesus), will teach you all things and will remind you of everything I (Jesus) have said to you."

All parts of the Trinity of God are omnipresent; that is, they can be in all places at one time. Psalm 139:8–12 says:

"If I go up to the heavens, you are there; if I make my bed in the depths, you are there. If I rise on the wings of the dawn, if I settle on the far side of the sea, even there your hand will hold me fast. If I say, 'Surely the darkness will hide me and the light become night around me,' even the darkness will not be dark to you; the night will shine like the day, for darkness is as light to you."

All three persons of the Trinity are omniscient; that is, they are all-knowing:

"For you created my inmost being; you knit me together in my mother's womb. I praise you because I am fearfully and wonderfully made; your works are wonderful, I know that full well. My frame was not hidden from you when I was made in the secret place. When I was woven together in the depths of the earth, your eyes saw my unformed body. All the days ordained for me were written in your book before one of them came to be." **– Psalm 137:13–16**

The Humbled and Exalted Christ

Apostle Paul wrote in **Philippians 2:5–11:**

> *"Let this mind be in you which was also in Christ Jesus, who being in the form of God, did not consider it robbery to be equal with God, but made Himself of no reputation, taking the form of a bondservant, and coming in the likeness of men. He (Jesus) humbled Himself and became obedient to the point of death, even the death of the cross. Therefore God also has highly exalted Him and given Him the name which is above every name, that at the name of Jesus every knee should bow, of those in Heaven, and of those on earth, and of those under the earth, and that every tongue should confess that Jesus Christ is Lord, to the glory of God the Father."*

Once again, it's so important to know that if Christ were not a Deity but just a man who lived a good life and gave us an exceptional example on how to live and forgive, our sin would still alienate us from God. It's of the utmost importance that we know for certain Christ is who He said He is. The Bible is absolutely clear in demonstrating the Deity of Christ. Why is the Deity of Christ so important? Because our place in eternity hinges on it. No religion except Christianity places such importance on the Deity of Christ (that He is fully God); the sinless God/Man is the foundation of our belief.

As the Apostle Paul points out when Deity comes back to earth in power and majesty, (that's the Christ described in **Revelation 1:12–18**): *"Every knee will bow and every tongue will confess. Jesus is Lord to the Glory of the Father"* **(Romans 14:11).** At this point, no unbelievers will remain on the earth; so every unbeliever will finally acknowledge the truth.

One time I was talking with a friend who said he didn't believe in God; not only that, he called himself an atheist, saying he didn't even believe God existed. I replied that on the day he died, he certainly would not be an atheist anymore and would have no excuse for his disbelief. **Romans 1:20** is very clear on that point: *"For since the creation of the world God's invisible qualities—his eternal power and divine nature—have been clearly seen, being understood from what has been made, so that people are without excuse."* There can be no manipulation of this verse's interpretation. Its simple but very frank meaning is that the atheist will stand without excuse before God—guilty of unbelief.

11

DOES SCIENCE ELIMINATE GOD?

Stephen Hawking said, "I think the universe was spontaneously created out of nothing, according to the laws of science."[xiii]

Now, I am a mechanic who likes to figure out how things work by their design and repair them, so I found this to be an interesting quote. The great thing is, once I have figured out how something works, it doesn't change unless the designer changes it. I guess that would be called the Laws of Mechanics, and those laws are easy to replicate, which makes it a law (from my understanding).

Replicability: Not only does a scientific theory have to be testable, but it has to be a test anyone can repeat and get the same results.

Stephen Hawking says that the universe was spontaneously created out of nothing, "according to the laws of science." If that were true, however, the meaning of the word "law" would have to change. The laws of science clearly state that a scientific theory has to be testable to have viability, but I don't know of anyone replicating the action of creating something from nothing.

The scientific society's name for the universe being created out of nothing is the Big Bang Theory, and since this theory cannot be proven by replicability—which is the scientific standard—it remains only a theory, even though many would like for us to believe it is fact. Nevertheless, those who wish to believe in the Big Bang Theory must believe by faith in what they can't substantiate through replication. Those who choose to believe in the Big Bang Theory while being convinced that believing in God is just a futile act of faith are being discriminatory. Whether you choose the Big Bang Theory or God, believing in either requires faith. It is my opinion that believing in *the God of the Bible* takes a lot less faith. Hopefully, by the time you're finished reading this book, you will agree.

It's hard for me to believe that we all came from nothing, with no designer or creator. I just can't muster up enough faith to believe that; it's simply too far-fetched. The complexities of human life alone are more than enough in my mind to point to a creator. So why do so many people like my friend and Dr. Hawking want to take God right out of the picture? I just don't know. Pride, maybe?

Dr. Hawking also says this in his book *Brief Answers to the Big Questions:* "One could define God as the embodiment of the laws of nature; however, this is not what most people would think of as God. They mean a human-like being, with whom one can have a personal relationship. When you look at the vast size of the universe, and **how insignificant and <u>accidental</u> human life is in it,** that seems most implausible. **It's my view that the simplest explanation is that there is no God. No one created the universe,** and no one directs our fate. This leads me to a **profound realization: there is probably no heaven and afterlife either.** I think a belief in an afterlife is just **wishful thinking.** There is no reliable evidence for it, and it flies in the face of everything we know in science. **I think that when we die we return to dust.** But there's a sense in which we live on, in our influence, and in our genes that we pass on to our children. We have this one life to **appreciate the grand design of the universe,** and for that I am extremely grateful."[xiv]

So, if we believe the statements Dr. Hawking has made, human life is accidental. And because of the vastness of the universe, we are so insignificant that God wouldn't want a relationship with us even if He did exist. I guess the notion that God would become flesh, dwell among us, and then die on the cross for our sins would be considered downright ludicrous in many scientists' eyes. If that's the way you want to see it, you have free will to see it that way. I, on the other hand, believe what the Bible says in **1 John 4:9**: *"God showed how much He loved us by sending His one and only Son into the world so that we might have eternal life through Him."*

That verse and many like it say we are absolutely not too insignificant for God to be in a relationship with us. According to the Bible, we have great worth in God's eyes, which I think is a far better reality than Dr. Hawking's views.

The concept of a loving God is nowhere to be found in what was quoted from Stephen Hawking's book *Brief Answers to the Big Questions*. What I ascertain from Stephen Hawking's quote about there being no God is that he does not believe in a Deity greater than himself. Trying to study the design of the universe by the laws of science, while not even acknowledging that there is a designer, isn't very analytical in my opinion. In fact, why would Hawking even see a designer when it seems that his whole goal is not to recognize one—especially a God who wants a relationship with His creation.

If we take a loving God out of the universe, we're left with a very cold existence without hope. Another major problem in believing there is no God is this: if we just descended from the animal kingdom or from a single cell, what chance does mankind have? Right and wrong are based on God's laws; remove God, and the standard for right and wrong can become skewed very quickly. I think we can already see the effects that moving away from God is having. I don't even care to watch the news anymore because of the blatant misrepresentation of the truth or the miscarriage of justice on a worldwide scale.

Dr. Hawking said, "I think that when we die, we return to dust."[xv] If this is the case, death becomes the ultimate end—no soul, no afterlife, nothing to comfort the bereaving. The bleakness of his statement can only breed an "all about me" or "grab all you can out of this life for there is nothing else" attitude in society. In fact, it already has. You can't even argue that point—just watch TV today to see how today's entitled generation is making out. Violence, sex, and lying are the major theme in ninety percent of its shows or movies.

Why is man searching out on such a broad scale what hurts us as a society and on an individual level what goes against everything God wants for us? The simple reason is that these are the attributes of the god of this world, Satan; and most have made Satan their god without even realizing it.

One thing Dr. Hawking says is, "We have this one life to **appreciate the grand design of the universe.**"[xvi] This is true, but better than that, if we don't take God out of the picture, we can appreciate the grand design of the universe and the designer Himself—God.

> *"For since the creation of the world God's invisible qualities—his eternal power and divine nature—have been clearly seen, being understood from what has been made, so that people are without excuse."* **– Romans 1:20**

It's very interesting that Dr. Hawking tells us to appreciate the grand design of the universe when he says that the universe was spontaneously created out of nothing. If something materialized out of nothing, where did the design come from? The complexities of the universe, as well as the complexities of life itself, warrant a designer—that is what logic dictates.

In the introduction, I made this similar statement: if I am wrong and Dr. Hawking is right, I have lost nothing. If I am right about God and Dr. Hawking is wrong, well, that's going to be tragic for a lot of people, especially those who believe Dr. Hawking's statement that there is no God.

I pray to God on my friend's behalf that he will work out in his heart why he has continuously chosen to deny God's existence. I hope he figures this out before he dies and bows his knee before Jesus as he awaits judgement upon his soul. I know this sounds harsh, but I didn't make up the rules. I do have to live by them, though, and I can't live by them if I disregard their existence.

Don't be swayed by Stephen Hawking or others regarding God's authenticity. Search it out for yourself.

Not knowing the whole story about my dad made him seem very harsh to me. Not knowing God or only believing the total misrepresentation of God's character by man-made religions doesn't seem justifiable. As I got to know my dad, my view of him changed; in the same way, your views will change when you get to know the one and only true God—*the God of the Bible*. We will never have all of the answers this side of Heaven, but we do have enough to be satisfied that God's character is trustworthy and above reproach.

Allow me to clarify that I in no way disregard the great mind of Dr. Hawking, and I mean no disrespect by disagreeing with his view that there is no God. I am merely giving my opinion from what I know to be true from the Bible—just as he gave his opinion on what he has decided to be true based on his knowledge of science. It's up to you, the reader, to determine which truth you choose to believe. Just be sure to take into consideration the implications of making the wrong choice since only one of these two positions is based on truth.

12

THE BIBLE

The Bible is the world's best-selling and most widely distributed book. It has been translated into 349 languages, and 2,123 people groups have at least one book of the Bible in their language. It is estimated that more than five billion copies have been printed. The Bible has definitely not lost its appeal.

Owning a Bible that is not being read is like having a box that contains the keys to all kinds of riches just collecting dust on a shelf. All of the riches of Heaven, love, and God are in the pages of the Bible, waiting for whoever reads it to believe it and receive its promises.

Dr. Jeremiah: Insight on the Bible

"It is the magnificent details of prophecies that mark the Bible as the inspired Word of God. Only God could foreknow and accomplish all that was written about Christ. This historical accuracy and reliability sets the Bible apart from any other book or record. **The Bible** is made up of sixty-six books and thirty-five different authors. Every word was penned by a person like you or me, yet each word was breathed out by God as holy men of old spoke as the **Holy Spirit** moved them. The resulting Book is unique, inspired, infallible, inerrant, never-failing, every-reviving, as old as antiquity, as relevant as tomorrow's headlines, and forever **established in Heaven** (*Understanding the 66 Books of the Bible,* Dr. David Jeremiah)."[xvii]

The Bible is one story from cover to cover, not many, like so many people believe. It was written from start to finish over 1500 years ago, and no piece of literature has ever existed where the message has remained so unchanged in its entirety.

It's about the good news of Jesus the Saviour, triumphant living, and achievements and failures. It's about life being exposed, mankind's total vulnerability and selfishness, and his fall from God's grace.

God didn't edit anything out; instead, it's a revealing account of our true nature, God's never-ending love for us, and His faithful pursuit to bring us to reconciliation, which is the restoration of a friendly relationship with Him through Jesus Christ. The Bible is the only instruction manual on how to be reconciled with God and to show us how to live a life pleasing to Him.

Though the Bible is a book of great love, it is also a book of warnings—one that tells us what happens when that great love is cast aside for worldly gratification instead of heavenly rewards.

What about Different Interpretations of the Bible?

It's crucial to remember that the Bible itself is the single best guide to its own interpretation. The infallible rule of interpretation of Scripture is Scripture itself; and therefore, when there is a question about the true interpretation of any Scripture, it should be validated by other Scripture in the Bible.

One other important thing to remember is that if you are having a difficult time with any piece of Scripture, sometimes finding out the history and culture of that time period provides clarity. Many times, our pastor would begin by explaining the historical and cultural background of the era in which the Scripture was written before teaching the passage. This helped me visualize in what context the Scripture was being used, making it easier to understand its interpretation. For example, later I explain how this method helped show the origin of the phrase "The Lamb of God."

One Interpretation Only

You and I could interpret places in Scripture differently, but certain subjects in Scripture are not open to debate—namely: Heaven and Hell, judgement, and Jesus Christ dying on the cross for our sins, being buried, and then rising again from the grave on the third day. The Scriptures that refer to Jesus and the events of His life are repeatedly validated by history, prophecy, and Scripture itself throughout the whole Bible. The Bible clearly describes the prophecies of Jesus the same way, from Genesis to Revelation.

Interpreting Scripture to Suit One's Lifestyle

At one point in my life, I had gotten away from God and was doing my own thing, living contrary to His Word. But I didn't try to justify my actions by rethinking the meaning of Scripture that didn't suit my sinful lifestyle. No, I would simply say, "I know what the Bible says, and at this time, I am not adhering to it." In the end, that came with some pretty heavy consequences, but more on that later.

Taking Scripture Out of Context

Bill followed a religion that was clearly taking parts of the Scripture out of context by using only a verse or two, or parts of a verse, to validate a certain interpretation or truth.

One night, I invited Bill over to discuss the Bible. I had one rule though: if we were going to quote Scripture, we had to read the five verses both before and after the quoted verse to ensure the interpretation wasn't being taken out of context.

As we started to discuss the different passages of Scripture throughout the Bible, this rule to validate Scripture worked great. We both agreed on many parts of the Bible until Bill started using single verses or parts of verses from different sections of the Bible to support his doctrinal beliefs. Using the five verses before and after method, his doctrine was unsupported by Scripture. The infallible rule of interpretation of Scripture is Scripture itself, and his doctrine could not withstand that rule.

Bill was a great guy, and I thoroughly enjoyed our evening of looking through the Bible together. Bill's knowledge of the Bible indicated that he read the Scriptures on a regular basis. But when he started to support his point of view by using verses or parts of verses out of context, I felt that he was deceiving himself

My prayer is that validating Scripture with Scripture results in Bill learning the value of incorporating that practice into his Bible studies. Reading God's Word on a regular basis and missing the intended truth is devastating in the end.

Some argue that Scripture has too many interpretations. If this is your reason for discarding its validity, that won't absolve you of your accountability for its content.

What is our accountability for knowing the content of what's in the Bible? One time, after I failed an English exam, the teacher asked why I had failed. I told her that I didn't really understand English that well and had better things to do than ask for help and study. Her reply was "That's okay, Mike. We will see you next year when you take my class over again." Failing an English course that I could take again is an inconvenience. Missing out on what the Bible says about God's plan of salvation is going to be a lot more inconvenient than you think, and make-up classes don't exist. It's a one-shot deal, so don't drop out; keep reading. God would like nothing more than for you to pass through to Heaven.

13

THE BIRTH OF DEITY

Christts, the God/Man

The birth of Jesus was foretold in **Luke 1:26–38:**

"In the sixth month of Elizabeth's pregnancy, (with John the Baptist) God sent the angel Gabriel to Nazareth, a town in Galilee, to a virgin pledged to be married to a man named Joseph, a descendant of David. The virgin's name was Mary. The angel went to her and said, 'Greetings, you who are highly favoured! The Lord is with you.' Mary was greatly troubled at his words and wondered what kind of greeting this might be. But the angel said to her, 'Do not be afraid, Mary; you have found favour with God. You will conceive and give birth to a son, and you are to call him Jesus. He will be great and will be called the Son of the Most High. The Lord God will give him the

throne of his father David, and he will reign over Jacob's descendants forever; his kingdom will never end.' 'How will this be,' Mary asked the angel, 'since I am a virgin?' The angel answered, 'The Holy Spirit will come on you, and the power of the Most High will overshadow you. So the holy one to be born will be called the Son of God. Even Elizabeth your relative is going to have a child in her old age, and she who was said to be unable to conceive is in her sixth month. For no word from God will ever fail.' 'I am the Lord's servant,' Mary answered. 'May your word to me be fulfilled.' Then the angel left her."

The virgin birth is the only way Christ could keep His Deity and be both God and man. As I mentioned before, since the fall in the Garden of Eden, humanity has been born into sin. So, if Christ was born from the seed of man, then He would have been born into sin like the rest of us. But Christ's birth, which was accomplished by the Holy Spirit through the Virgin Mary, came from above, making Jesus the sinless **Lamb of God.**

Disputing the virgin birth of Jesus means that you are disputing the power of God. God isn't an old guy in a rocking chair looking down from Heaven, stroking his white beard and pondering all that has gone wrong in the world. But as **Matthew 19:26** says, God is the God of the impossible: *"Jesus looked at them and said, 'With man this is impossible, but with God all things are possible.'"*

All things are possible, and that's why I believe in an all-powerful God—one that made the heavens and earth in six days and then rested on the seventh, holding the whole universe together in His hand. He is a God that is not limited by anything, a righteous and just God who loved us so much that He gave us not only free will, but also an escape from judgement even if we use our free will to sin at His expense. If I am going to follow a god, I want to follow the all-powerful God—*the God of the Bible*.

In essence, if no virgin birth had occurred, then Christ's work on the cross would be null and void. This is because the only way the atonement for our sins could satisfy God was if the offering for sin was from a perfect/sinless man, and man is neither perfect nor sinless. But thanks be to God, Jesus Christ is.

14

THE LAMB OF GOD

An Offering for Humanity's Sin

Why was a sin offering necessary? Because without the shedding of blood, there can be no forgiveness of sin or atonement.

Atonement is the process of causing an offence to be forgiven or pardoned (acquitted). The offence we need atonement for is that we were born into sin, which has separated us from God. To be forgiven, or pardoned, the debt of sin has to be paid. This is why Christ willingly went to the cross: to sacrifice His life as payment for our sin and offer that payment as a gift to all those who would believe.

In plain terms, we have assumed a debt from past generations, which we have added to, but can't pay. The law states that anyone who has defaulted on a debt with no means to pay it back has to be punished and banished from the community forever. But there is one who has great wealth along with compassion on the debtor, and He takes the punishment for the debt. In turn, the debt is paid and forgotten; we are accepted back into the community—now reconciled. **In Biblical terms,** the debt is sin, the compassionate one is Jesus Christ, the punishment is banishment to Hell, and the payment is Christ's death on the cross—Christ's sacrificial offering for sin.

Hebrews 9:22 tells us God's law requires an offering for sin: a blameless animal with no defects. *"In fact, the law requires that nearly everything be cleansed with blood, and without the shedding of blood there is no forgiveness."*

In the Old Testament, the sacrifices of animals provided only a temporary atonement (payment) for sins—like a down-payment—until Christ's sacrifice. Christ's sacrifice was a one-time payment for all sin, which cleansed all who believed of their sinfulness before God.

These sacrifices of animals in the Old Testament and the sacrifice of Christ on the cross in the New Testament seems very barbaric to me because I don't view sin as God does. I also don't see the seriousness of sin like a Holy God. But trying to understand why God uses blood to cleanse sin, and that there is no forgiveness without the shedding of blood, will hopefully open our eyes to the severity of sin. It's a hard concept to grasp for sure, but it is the basis for our atonement (the reconciliation of God and mankind through Jesus Christ).

I have a hard time understanding why Christ had to be that sacrifice in the first place, but just because I have a hard time understanding these things doesn't mean I am not accountable to search it out and find clarity on the subject. I just can't throw my hands in the air and walk away as Pontius Pilate, the Roman Governor of Judaea, tried to do when they brought Jesus to him.

Jesus Before Pilate

Matthew 27:11–26 tells the story of when Jesus, an innocent man, stood before Pontius Pilate. Why was Jesus brought before Pilate by the chief priests? Because Jesus claimed to be God, which was blasphemy—a crime punishable by death in those days. But the priests did not have the authority to execute Jesus; they had to get that permission from the Roman governor.

Standing before Pontius Pilate, the man who had the power to release him, Jesus was asked to give a response to the accusation brought against him by the chief priests; but Jesus refused to answer. Pilate could find no fault in Jesus, so was amazed by Jesus' lack of response to defend Himself, which was a fulfillment of Old Testament prophecy: *"He was oppressed and afflicted, yet he did not open his mouth; he was led like a lamb to the slaughter, and as a sheep before its shearers is silent, so he did not open his mouth"* **(Isaiah 53:7).**

Pilate could have released Jesus right then but decided instead to take a bowl of water and wash his hands before the crowd of Jews waiting to see if they were allowed to have Jesus put to death. Pilate declared in front of everyone that he was washing his hands of this man's blood: *"I am innocent of this man's blood, take Him, He is your responsibility."* Basically, he was telling the priests that they had the freedom to do whatever they wanted with Jesus, so they crucified Him on a cross.

Pilate's symbolic action didn't absolve him of his duties as a government official to do what was right in the eyes of the Lord or of Christ's blood, which is still on his hands today. Pilate could have taken the time to find out who Jesus really was and chosen a different course of action, but he didn't; he was swayed and bullied by the crowd. Pilate's chance for redemption has long since passed, but for us, as long as we still have breath in our lungs, we still have the opportunity to find out who Jesus really is. Finding out who Jesus is can change your life here on earth and determine where you will spend eternity.

For the last two thousand years, Pontius Pilate has been awaiting judgement in a place where he wishes he wasn't, thinking of all the things he should have done differently when it came to his dealings with Jesus Christ. To add salt to the wound, he didn't listen to his wife's advice when she sent him a message to leave Jesus alone. **Matthew 27:19** documents the message she sent: *"While Pilate was sitting on the judge's seat, his wife sent him this message: 'Don't have anything to do with that innocent man.'"* God warned Pilate through his wife, but he didn't listen. And for the last two thousand years, he has most certainly been wishing that he had.

God warns us by the convicting powers of the Holy Spirit what we should do with Jesus. I have always found it a good idea to learn from others' mistakes and avoid stepping into the same bucket of woes myself. The account of Pontius Pilate's dealing with Christ the wrong way would be a good bucket to avoid.

When I die, I don't want to be awaiting judgement in a place I wish I wasn't, with a clear understanding that I deserve to be there. That is why I have accepted Jesus' offer of salvation now, rather than waiting until "later"—because "later" has a way of never coming to pass.

The Lamb of God

Where did the term *the Lamb of God* come from? It's documented in the Book of Exodus that the Egyptians used the Israelites as slaves for about 400 years. This took place around 1400 years before the birth of Christ (BC). The Israelites had been petitioning God for someone to deliver them from the hands of the Egyptians, and God answered by choosing Moses. But Pharaoh, the ruler of Egypt, would not let them go. God sent plagues on the land to change Pharaoh's mind, but that only hardened Pharaoh's heart to resist Moses' requests.

The last plague that was sent to change Pharaoh's mind, which succeeded, was recorded in **Exodus 12:12**. A plague of death was pronounced upon all the firstborn in Egypt, both people and animals.

> *"On that same night I will pass through Egypt and strike down every firstborn of both people and animals, and I will bring judgment on all the gods of Egypt. I am the Lord. The blood will be a sign for you on the houses where you are, and when I see the blood, I will pass over you. No destructive plague will touch you when I strike Egypt."*

If a one-year-old male lamb or goat, without defect, was slain and some of its blood was applied to the sides and tops of the doorframes of the house, this was a sign to the angel of death to pass over that house and spare the firstborn from death. This event was known as The Passover. **The imagery of the Passover would be applied to Christ. He would become the Passover Lamb, the Lamb of God whose blood would once and for all cleanse us from the sinfulness that separated us from God.**

Why is it so important to connect Old Testament events to the New Testament? It helps give clarification to who Christ is and what He did on the cross. Without a good understanding of Christ and the written account leading up to His death and after, you can't really be sure to whom you're giving your allegiance.

Many people will believe in just about anything today, following blindly and without understanding. An example of this is the saying: "It doesn't matter what you believe, as long as you believe, and it makes you happy." That statement is just plain absurd. It very much matters what you believe and the reasoning behind that belief. A strong foundation to a belief system gives strength in times of trouble and empowers you to stand up for what you believe—even in the face of intimidation or persecution.

Comprehension of the things of God gives assurance to anyone committing themselves to Jesus Christ that He can be trusted with our lives. Faith and knowledge go hand in hand, making a good foundation for the believer. Some would say believing in the Gospel of Christ is intellectual suicide—a crutch for the weak-minded. I totally disagree. Being connected to God, the sovereign Master of the universe through the empowerment of the Holy Spirit, gives greater knowledge and understanding about God, life, why we are here, where we are going when we die, and the world in which we live. For God said in **Proverbs**

2:6, *"For the Lord gives wisdom; from his mouth comes knowledge and understanding."*

It's amazing to me, as humans stumble onto uncovering how some of God's creation works, that those who essentially have figured it out using their own intellect, have ruled out the necessity for a God out of their own conceit. They pridefully say, "Look at us: look at how smart we are." In later pages, we will see how God addresses Job on the subject of man's understanding of God's ways and how He runs His universe.

John the Baptist

John the Baptist was the child of a priest named Zachariah and his wife, Elizabeth. Both were advanced in years, which made John's birth a miracle of God. The Angel of the Lord gave Mary the news about Jesus and John the Baptist. *"Now indeed, Elizabeth your relative has also conceived a son in her old age; and this is now the sixth month for her who was called barren. For with God nothing will be impossible"* **(Luke 1:36–37).**

John the Baptist's ministry was to prepare the way for the Lord, meaning that he pointed the people of his time to Christ, the Lamb of God, the one who would redeem mankind.

> *"As it is written in Isaiah **(Isaiah 40:3)** the prophet, 'Behold, I send my messenger (John the Baptist) before your face, who will prepare Your (Christ) way; The voice of one crying in the wilderness, make ready the way of the Lord, make His paths straight.' John the Baptist appeared in the wilderness preaching a baptism of repentance*

for the forgiveness of sins. (7) And he was preaching, and saying, 'After me One (Jesus) is coming who is mightier than I, and I am not fit to stoop down and untie the thong of his sandals.'"
– Mark 1:2–4, 7

John the Baptist sure knew the Deity of Christ.

The Lamb of God (Jesus Christ)

"But with the precious blood of Christ, a lamb without blemish or defect." **– 1 Peter 1:19**

"The next day John saw Jesus coming toward him and said, 'Look, the Lamb of God, who takes away the sin of the world! This is the one I meant when I said, A man who comes after me has surpassed me because he was before me.'" **– John 1:29–30**

This is where the imagery of the Passover lamb written about in the Old Testament Book of Exodus comes to life in describing Christ in the New Testament. This Lamb of God was Jesus in the flesh, the only one worthy to be sacrificed for the payment for man's sin. Just as when the angel of death in Moses' time needed to see sacrificed blood on the doorpost to pass over the house, God needs to see us washed with Christ's blood (figuratively) to credit His righteousness onto us, so that when God looks at us, He sees no sin, and we escape judgement by His grace. No one will ever pass through Heaven's gates without having his or her sin washed away by the sacrificial blood of Christ.

Good News

Jesus, who was called the Lamb of God, was the perfect and final sacrifice for sin—Jesus went to the cross on our behalf, so all who come to Him by faith will be saved by His righteousness. When cloaked in the righteousness of Jesus, we are forgiven and made right in God's eyes. Jesus was the last sacrifice needed for the sins of man, as **Hebrews 10:11–18** states:

> *"Day after day every priest stands and performs his religious duties; again and again he offers the same sacrifices, which can never take away sins. But when this priest (Jesus) had offered for all time one sacrifice for sins, He (Jesus) sat down at the right hand of God, and since that time He (Jesus) waits for his enemies to be made his footstool. For by one sacrifice He (Jesus) has made perfect forever those who are being made holy. The Holy Spirit also testifies to us about this. First he says: 'This is the covenant I will make with them after that time, says the Lord. I will put my laws in their hearts, and I will write them on their minds.' Then he adds: 'Their sins and lawless acts I will remember no more.' And where these have been forgiven, sacrifice for sin is no longer necessary."*

The Blood of Christ

Let me try to bring this into perspective, for the sacrifices of animals and using their blood as a symbolic action to wash away sins cannot get any more foreign to us. But when trying to come to grips with this analogy, we always have to remember that the way we look at sin and the way a holy God looks at sin are farther from each other than we can imagine.

Sin has such a devastating effect on all of us. To God it has to be dealt with before any relationship with Him can be re-established. To God, the severity of sin means something must die so the other can live. Christ had to die so that we could live. By the shedding of Christ's blood (at His death), and then His resurrection, we can receive God's gift of forgiveness and enter into an agreement with God that says, when He looks at us, He sees the righteousness of His Son (Jesus) and not our sin anymore, thus restoring our relationship. This agreement is sealed or notarized by Christ's blood, verifying it's legally binding forever. Notarization is the official fraud deterrent process that assures the parties of a transaction that a document is authentic and can be trusted.

The Banishment

In the example below, I am in no way trying to disrespect or downplay the seriousness of what Christ went through on the cross, but allow me to offer a simplistic example of why we need to have our sins washed away by Christ's blood.

I was walking through the park late one night with my dog, Lucky. Since no one was around, he was off his leash, running around with his nose to the ground, drawn by every new smell. I was a little distracted, for these late-night walks were my time to think and pray. Periodically, I would look over to see what Lucky was doing. One of those times, I saw him heading full speed toward something in the field by the tree line. Thinking it was a rabbit, I wasn't too concerned for the rabbit, since Lucky had never been able to catch one before. But as he drew closer to his intended target, I noticed that what he was charging wasn't moving away. I quickly yelled at him to heel, which means stop and return to my side immediately. Lucky did not obey, and a moment later I heard a yelp, followed by my big, black Labrador retriever heading back towards me with his tail between his legs. The wind was behind him and in seconds I smelt the strong odour of a dog that had just been sprayed by a skunk at close range.

Here is the simplistic similarity between our sin and the skunk spray:

Lucky was contaminated; the smell was overwhelming, and he was no longer welcomed or even let back into our home. In fact, he was banished to his outside doghouse. He was ostracized from everyone, and even the sad look on his face didn't melt anyone's heart enough to venture near him. If only he had listened to my command to heel and returned to my side, all of this could have been avoided. Lucky knew better than to disobey my commands; even though he is a dog, he knew there would be consequences. But off his leash, he had freedom, and he used that freedom to disobey me; and the repercussion of that act of disobedience was no fellowship with the master he loved or anyone else for that matter.

The Restoration

Being the loving master I am, and needing to fix the problem of the smelly dog, I went to the supermarket the next morning and purchased many large cans of tomato juice. Once home, I scrubbed that poor dog within an inch of his life with that blood red juice until all the smell was out of his fur.

Once cleaned, he was welcome back into our home, fellowship was restored, and once again his tail wagged furiously when he met me at the door when I returned home from work—all was good.

When we are cleansed by Christ's blood, our sin and its stench is gone. We are welcomed into the family of God, and our relationship is restored—all is good!

15

PROPHECIES

*"And I will put enmity between you (Satan) and
the woman, and between your offspring and hers,
he (Christ) will crush your head and you (Satan)
will strike his heel."* – **Genesis 3:15**

God First Spoke about Christ's Coming in Genesis

E
nmity or hostility will always exist between the offspring
of those who oppose Christ and those who follow Him.
The prophecy part of this verse is that Christ will deal a
death blow to Satan's head at the cross, while Satan will strike
Christ's heel (cause Him to suffer).

Satan thought he had won the battle by killing Christ on the
cross, but Christ's resurrection from the dead, was a death blow
to Satan's power. Now there is no fear in death for those who
choose to believe in Jesus Christ.

It's exciting that God talks about the good news of Christ right after the fall of mankind in Genesis. We are not going be left for dead in our sins. It's also very exciting that the prophesy in Genesis is verified by Isaiah's prophesy about Christ's coming in greater detail. This prophesy below was written by the Prophet Isaiah in the Old Testament over seven hundred years after the Genesis prophecy and about seven hundred years before Christ's birth.

Prophecies of Christ from Isaiah

"Who has believed our message and to whom has the arm of the Lord been revealed? He (Christ) grew up before him like a tender shoot, and like a root out of dry ground. He had no beauty or majesty to attract us to him, nothing in his appearance that we should desire him. He was despised and rejected by mankind, a man of suffering, and familiar with pain. Like one from whom people hide their faces he was despised, and we held him in low esteem. Surely he took up our pain and bore our suffering, yet we considered him punished by God, stricken by him, and afflicted. But he was pierced for our transgressions, he was crushed for our iniquities; the punishment that brought us peace was on him, and by his wounds we are healed. We all, like sheep, have gone astray, each of us has turned to our own way; and the Lord has laid on him the

iniquity of us all. He was oppressed and afflicted, yet he did not open his mouth; he was led like a lamb to the slaughter, and as a sheep before its shearers is silent, so he did not open his mouth. By oppression and judgment he was taken away. Yet who of his generation protested? For he was cut off from the land of the living; for the transgression of my people he was punished. He was assigned a grave with the wicked, and with the rich in his death, though he had done no violence, nor was any deceit in his mouth. Yet it was the Lord's will to crush him and cause him to suffer, and though the Lord makes his life an offering for sin, he will see his offspring and prolong his days, and the will of the Lord will prosper in his hand. After he has suffered, he will see the light of life and be satisfied; by his knowledge my righteous servant will justify many; and he will bear their iniquities. Therefore I will give him a portion among the great, and he will divide the spoils with the strong, because he poured out his life unto death, and was numbered with the transgressors. For he (Christ) bore the sin of many, and made intercession for the transgressors. " – **Isaiah 53:1–12**

(Verification of these prophecies by New Testament Scriptures is given in the appendix chapter, titled "Fulfillment of Prophecies," toward the back of the book.)

The Accuracy of Bible Prophecies

Isaiah 53 is one of the most descriptive prophecies concerning Christ's coming and dying for our sin from the approximately 300 prophecies in the Old Testament concerning Him. That's why we often find statements like this: *"These things happened so that the scripture would be fulfilled,"* in the writings of the New Testament **(John 19:36).** The fulfilment of Old Testament prophecies in the New Testament were not hit or miss but were absolutely accurate.

"For prophecy never had its origin in the human will, but prophets, though human, spoke from God as they were carried along by the Holy Spirit" **(2 Peter 1:21).**

The number of prophecies about Christ's coming and the total accuracy of those prophecies are amazing. Mathematically speaking, the odds of anyone fulfilling this number of prophecies are staggering. Mathematicians put it this way:

- 1 person fulfilling 8 prophecies: 1 chance in 100,000,000,000,000,000
- 1 person fulfilling 48 prophecies: 1 chance in 10 to the 157th power
- 1 person fulfilling 300+ prophecies: **Only Jesus**

Why is this information relevant? Anyone with a discerning mind must concede that all the prophecies written about Christ in the Old Testament that were fulfilled to the letter prove that He is who Scripture says He is. The prophecies regarding the first coming of Christ were absolutely fulfilled to the letter. This is just further reason to believe that the many prophecies about the second coming of Christ will also be fulfilled to the letter.

16

THE CROSS

The Final One-Time Payment for Sin

You **might wonder whether Jesus had no physical choice about going to the cross.** In other words, when the large crowd armed with swords and clubs, sent from the chief priests and elders came to forcibly arrest Jesus, did He have any other option but to go with them? The Bible is clear He did, for when the crowd came forward to take Jesus, Peter His disciple, pulled out his sword and struck the servant of the high priest cutting off his ear, then Jesus said to Peter: *Do you think I cannot call on my Father, and He will at once put at my disposal more than twelve legions of angels?* **– Matthew 26:53**

Let's look at how powerful an angel of the Lord is, as documented in **2 Kings 19:35** when the Assyrians came up against Israel: *"That night the angel of the Lord went out and put to death a hundred and eighty-five thousand in the Assyrian* *camp. When the people got up the next morning—behold all of them were dead."*

Why is this information important? Because Christ was not bound by anything other than His love for us and His commitment to doing the will of His Father. He suffered for us because of what was written in **Hebrews 12:2:** *"For the joy set before him he endured the cross, scorning its shame, and sat down at the right hand of the throne of God."*

John MacArthur Explains 2 Corinthians 5:21

2 Corinthians 5:21 tells us:

> *"God made him who had no sin to be sin for us, so that in him we might become the righteousness of God."*

MacArthur explains, "Christ was not made a sinner, nor was He punished for any sin of His own. Instead, the Father treated Him as if He were a sinner by charging to His account the sins of everyone who would ever believe. All those sins were charged against Him as if He had personally committed them, and He was punished with the penalty for them on the cross, experiencing the full fury of God's wrath unleashed against them all. It was at that moment that…'Jesus cried out with a loud voice, saying…My God, My God, why have You forsaken Me?' **(Matthew 27:46).** It is crucial, therefore, to understand that the only sense in which Jesus was made sin was by substitution. He was personally pure, yet officially deserving of blame; personally holy, yet legally guilty. But in dying on the cross, Christ did not become evil like we are, nor do redeemed sinners become inherently as holy as He is. God credits believers' sin to Christ's account, and His righteousness to theirs. Imputation is the key; if Christ was not fully righteous in His sacrificial death, we can't be considered fully righteous in the eyes of God. If Christ wasn't completely sinless, there is no hope of reconciliation for us."[xviii]

The Good News is that Christ was fully righteous and completely sinless and able to reconcile us to God the Father.

Surrendering to the Cross

Christ's acceptance of the cross was God's ultimate expression of boundless love and grace towards us. (Note that *acceptance* is a word indicating choice.)

The Soldiers Mock Jesus

> *"Then the governor's soldiers took Jesus into the Praetorium and gathered the whole company of soldiers around him. They stripped him and put a scarlet robe on him, and then twisted together a crown of thorns and set it on his head. They put a staff in his right hand. Then they knelt in front of him and mocked him. 'Hail, king of the Jews!' they said. They spit on him, and took the staff and struck him on the head again and again. After they had mocked him, they took off the robe and put his own clothes on him. Then they led him away to crucify him"* – **Matthew 27:27–31**

Jesus willingly endured mockery, beatings, and the shame of the cross: don't misconstrue love for weakness or surrendering for powerlessness—for it is just the opposite. Christ yielding to the cross was derived from immeasurable strength, and His surrendering to the cross was derived from boundless compassion. Jesus Christ was the strongest man that ever walked on the face of the earth because of His commitment to follow through with the Father's plan, even though He had the authority to display great power and judgement. At any time, Jesus could have called down thousands of angels and, in seconds, the entire human race would have ceased to exist. Instead, He endured the cross out of His perfect love towards us. How do we respond to such love as a whole? Mostly with utter indifference. Just look at how much homage the world pays to the True God today.

The Jewish religious leaders judged and condemned an innocent man to death. They beat and then hung Him on a cross to die between two criminals. "King of the Jews," the words inscribed on the cross itself announced His supposed crime. If it had ended there, that would have been beyond tragic; **but after three days, Christ was raised from the dead.**

Consider the wonder of it: "God determined that He would rather go to Hell on our behalf than live in Heaven without us. He so much wants us not to go to Hell that he paid a horrible price on the cross so that we wouldn't have to. As it stands, however, apart from Christ, our eternal future will be spent in Hell" (Larry Alcorn, author of *Heaven*).[xix]

The Apostle Paul wrote in **1 Corinthians 15:3–5:**

> *"For what I received I passed on to you as of first*
> *importance: that Christ died for our sins*
> *according to the Scriptures, that he was buried,*

that he was raised on the third day according to the Scriptures, and that he appeared to Cephas, and then to the Twelve (disciples)."

Please don't downplay the brutality of the cross. If I wrote out in detail, from His arrest to the beatings and everything else done to Him, you would find it gross, disgusting, repulsive, and sickening, to say the least. It's just something we do not want to think about in descriptive detail, but it did happen; and it was horrendous. The crucifixion was done by us as a human race, and Christ died for us to render God's grace through His work on that cross to all who believe.

After Jesus Was Raised from the Dead

1 Corinthians 15:55–57 says this about death: *"Where, O death, is your victory? Where, O death, is your sting? The sting of death is sin, and the power of sin is the law. But thanks be to God! He gives us the victory through our Lord Jesus Christ."*

Spiritual Death Can Be Avoided

Heaven's doors are open wide for all those who believe in their heart what is written in **Romans 10:8–10** and act upon it. But what does it say?

> *" 'The word is near you; it is in your mouth and in your heart,' that is, the message concerning faith that we proclaim: If you declare with your mouth, 'Jesus is Lord,' and believe in your heart that God raised him from the dead, you will be saved. For it is with your heart that you believe and are*

justified, and it is with your mouth that you profess your faith and are saved."

The Message of the Cross: Foolishness

In **1 Corinthians 1:18** the Apostle Paul puts it this way:

"For the message of the cross is foolishness to those who are perishing, but to us who are being saved it is the power of God. For it is written: 'I will destroy the wisdom of the wise; the intelligence of the intelligent I will frustrate.'"

After you read the verses that have been laid out here, what are your thoughts? Is it foolishness or a powerful message of redemption?

From my human perspective, it does seem foolish and hard to make sense of blood sacrifices, Satan, the battle for our souls, Hell and suffering, and God becoming flesh and letting His creation get the better of Him. Why should I believe it? Because back when I was a hurting twelve-year-old after my brother was killed in a car accident, I asked God, from my heart, for some type of answers that only He could give. Because of that prayer, over the years **Matthew 7:7** became a fulfillment: *"Ask and it will be given to you; seek and you will find; knock and the door will be opened to you."* And the door that was opened to me was clarity about who Jesus was and the fact that the cross on which He was sacrificed was not foolishness, but a powerful message of redemption.

Christ's Crucifixion: God's Powerful Gift of Love to the Undeserving

*"But God demonstrates His own love for us in this: While we were still sinners, Christ died for us." – **Romans 5:8***

Again, **1 Corinthians 1:18** is significant enough to repeat: *"For the message of the cross is foolishness to those who are perishing, but to us who are being saved it is the power of God."*

If you believe in the message of the cross and accept Christ's gift of redemption and become saved, you will find no foolishness in the message of the cross. You will discover only grace upon grace.

17

THE HOLY SPIRIT AND SALVATION

The Convicting Power of the Holy Spirit

"The convicting power of the Holy Spirit opens our eyes to our sin and opens our hearts to receive God's grace. The Holy Spirit shows us the crucifixion of Christ is not foolishness but the power of God to redeem us. When the Holy Spirit convicts people of their sin, He represents the righteous judgement of God. There is no appeal of this verdict. The Holy Spirit not only convicts people of sin, but He also brings them to repentance. The Holy Spirit brings to light our relationship to God. The convicting power of the Holy Spirit opens our eyes to our sin and opens our hearts to receive God's grace. We praise the Lord for the Holy Spirit's conviction of sin and the restoring of our heart to God. For no one is brought to salvation apart from the work of the Holy Spirit. The Bible teaches that all people are by nature rebels against God and hostile to Jesus Christ. They are *'dead in trespasses and sins'* **(Ephesians 2:1)**. Jesus said, *'No one can come to Me unless the Father who sent Me draws him'* **(John 6:44)**. Part of that 'draw' to Jesus is the conviction of sin" **(gotquestions.org)**.[xx]

Are We, by Nature, Really Rebels?

It's very hard for most of us to think we are rebels against God and hostile to Jesus Christ, but I can't stress this enough. What is important is only what God thinks, and the only place to find out what God thinks is in the Holy Bible. Thankfully, His grace gives the Holy Spirit to help us discern what the Bible says. If the Bible says those who do not believe in Jesus Christ as God prescribes in the Bible are rebels against God and hostile to Jesus Christ, then they are. Can you believe and serve God and still be a rebel towards Him? Many serve God for the wrong reasons, which they deem right, so are still considered by God to be "rebels and hostile" towards Him.

As **Proverbs 14:12** points out, *"Before every man there lies a wide and pleasant road that seems right but ends in death."* I have heard it said many times that all roads lead to God if you are spiritual; that is a "broad, wide and pleasant" thought, but "ends in death." Why? It's very simple. Because of pride, people want to find their own way to God outside of what the Bible and Jesus Himself say—is the way. Jesus reiterates **Proverbs 14:12** in **Matthew 7:13** when He says, *"Enter through the narrow gate.*

For wide is the gate and broad is the road that leads to destruction (Hell), *and many enter through it."*

Why would Jesus make that statement if it wasn't true? It's a warning that what seems right to many is not necessarily the right way. We need the Holy Spirit's convicting power to show us that we need to come to God. To say it again: without the conviction of sin, there can be no salvation. Don't be fooled into thinking that you or I have a good standing before God. In our own strength, that will never be true—in our own strength, we are on the "wide and pleasant road that leads to destruction."

Conviction of My Sinfulness

Why did I become aware that the conviction of the Holy Spirit was true towards me? Because God puts in our consciousness that He is who He said He is, whether we want to acknowledge it or not.

> *"For since the creation of the world God's invisible qualities—his eternal power and divine nature—have been clearly seen, being understood from what has been made, so that people are without excuse. For although they knew God, they neither glorified him as God nor gave thanks to him, but their thinking became futile and their foolish hearts were darkened." –* **Romans 1:20– 21**

The consciousness that God instilled into all of mankind that He is the one and only true God, got all screwed up in my life at first because of my pride and sinful nature. My thinking became futile, and my heart was darkened by going through life just thinking that there was a God and that was good enough.

By not searching out God, I was saying that Michael Borthwick was his own god, determining his own fate—as if I have much control over my own life or the next beat of my heart and the next breath I take. After quite a few brushes with death over the years, especially in my motorcycling years, I now have an unmistakable awareness that my allotted days here on earth are totally in God's hands and His hands only. On that revelation, I finally humbled myself before God.

Salvation is moving head knowledge to heart knowledge. So, I came to believe in the one and only God of the Bible. I believe in the Deity of Jesus Christ. I believe that Jesus Christ was the Word of God made flesh who died on the cross for my sins. He was raised from the dead on the third day and now sits at the right hand of God. I believe it all, but the question that was put to me by God was this: now that you have knowledge, what are you going to do with it?

My head knowledge was the accumulation of Biblical facts, comparable to memorizing mathematical equations. The heart knowledge would be using those mathematical equations to build something amazing. In the same way, I had to take my biblical knowledge of God and use it from a heart perspective to change my thinking: not to trust in my own righteousness for salvation, but to trust only in Jesus' amazing gift of salvation through His righteousness.

As I said in the early part of my testimony, I was very aware that not making a decision was going to be considered rejection on my part. The Holy Spirit showed me the foolishness of my thinking, and I went from having a foolish and darkened heart to an enlightened heart, by asking Jesus' for forgiveness by faith and accepting His gift of salvation.

Faith is the adhesive that bonds us together with Jesus for eternity.

Hebrews 11:16 puts it best:

> *"And without faith it is impossible to please God, because anyone who comes to him must believe that he exists and that he rewards those who earnestly seek him."*

My Prayer

How did I make that decision by faith? I moved that head knowledge to heart knowledge and accepted Christ's offer of grace through prayer. I prayed the sinner's prayer from my heart: I acknowledged I was a sinner, deserving punishment for my sinfulness, and that nothing I could do on my own could rectify that. I believe Jesus is God and lived a sinless life. I placed my trust totally in what Jesus did on the cross, acknowledging Him as my newly found Saviour, making Him Lord of my life from that moment on. I asked Him to guide my life and help me to do His will (become more like Him). I prayed this in the name of Jesus.

With that, I became a born-again Christian. Nothing else had to be done; my salvation was complete and my journey to Heaven was bought and paid for by Christ Himself.

Luke 15:10 tells what a big deal it is to God and the host of Heaven when someone repents and comes to Jesus Christ: *"In the same way there is joy in the presence of the angels of God when one sinner repents."* Notice the phrase, *"when one sinner repents."* **Repentance** is a 180-degree turn towards God, leaving the old and bringing in the new; not living for self, but for God. And that is exactly what I have been doing since I accepted Christ, and also telling others the exciting news about my salvation. Jesus is speaking in **Matthew 10:23**: *"If anyone publicly acknowledges me (Jesus) before people, I also will acknowledge him before my Father who is in Heaven."*

The Work of the Holy Spirit

Nothing can or will thwart my final destination. Eternal security is mine; it is secured by the same Holy Spirit who dwells in the heart of every true believer.

"The **Holy Spirit** is not an 'it'. The Holy Spirit is a Person. The Bible says that He is not something, He is Someone. He is God. There are three Persons in the Trinity—God the Father, God the Son and God the Holy Spirit (Billy Graham)."[xxi]

First, the work of the Holy Spirit, as said before, is to convict us of our sin. *"And when He (Holy Spirit) has come, He will convict the world of sin, and of righteousness and judgment"* **(John 16:8).** Without the work of the Holy Spirit, we could never have our sins forgiven. We could never be saved. We could never go to Heaven. And that is why, when searching out God, a prayer from the heart compels the Holy Spirit to work in our lives.

Second, the Holy Spirit gives new life. *"Unless one is born again, he cannot see the kingdom of God"* **(John 3:3).** You must be born again. And the Holy Spirit is the One who does the work of making you a born-again person. It is a supernatural act, sealed by the Holy Spirit for the day of redemption—the day when we are free from this body of sin and receive our new sinless body like the resurrected Christ.

Third, the Holy Spirit indwells us. *"Do you not know that you are the temple of God and that the Spirit of God dwells in you?"* **(1 Corinthians 3:16).** The moment we accept Christ by faith, the Holy Spirit makes a forever home in our hearts. He gives us the power to serve Christ. *"You shall receive power when the Holy Spirit comes upon you; and you shall be witnesses to Me"* **(Acts 1:8).** The Holy Spirit gives us the power to love and serve Christ. Serving Christ is the greatest evidence to all that know you that your life has changed for God.

Fourth, the Holy Spirit produces in us the fruit of the Spirit. *"But when the Holy Spirit controls our lives He will produce this kind of fruit in us: love, joy, peace, longsuffering, kindness, goodness, faithfulness, gentleness and self-control"* **(Galatians 5:22–23).** You may be thinking you know some Christians who are not displaying that fruit. The key words in this verse are, *"when the Holy Spirit controls our lives."* We didn't give up our free will at salvation. It's a choice in all areas of our Christian lives as to how much control we give to the Holy Spirit. I can testify in my own life that the more control I give to the Spirit of God, the less inner turmoil I have, and the more love I show. This makes my walk with the Lord a joyful experience.

Fifth, the Holy Spirit has all knowledge. The Bible says in **1 Corinthians 2:10,** *"But we know about these things because God has sent his Spirit to tell us, and His Spirit searches out and shows us all of God's deepest secrets."* I can testify to this also, for before I was saved, reading the Bible was hard and it didn't make sense to me. Now when I read God's Word, the pages come alive—the meanings in Scripture speak to my heart and the truths become part of who I am.

2 Corinthians 3:14 says:

> *"Because they cannot see and understand the real meaning of the Scriptures. For this veil of misunderstanding can be removed only by believing in Christ."*

Sixth, the Holy Spirit is the only protection we have against evil. *"For our struggle is not against flesh and blood, but against the authorities, against the powers of this dark world and against the spiritual forces of evil in the heavenly realms"* **(Ephesians 6:12).** This means that evil forces in the world get into men's hearts and cause havoc beyond comprehension. The Holy Spirit limits the forces of evil at this present time, but there will be a day when those who are born again will be taken up from the earth in a moment, along with the Holy Spirit, this event is called the rapture. That day, Satan will no longer be held at bay—which is surely not a time when you would want to be left behind.

> *"For the Lord himself will come down from heaven, with a loud command, with the voice of the archangel and with the trumpet call of God,*

and the dead in Christ will rise first. After that, we
who are still alive and are left will be caught up
together with them in the clouds to meet the Lord
in the air." – **1 Thessalonians 4:16–17**

When the rapture occurs as stated in the verses above, the Holy Spirit's influence will be removed from the earth.

1 Thessalonians 2:7 tells us what that will look like: *"For the secret power of lawlessness* (anarchy, chaos, rebellion) *is already at work; but the one* (Holy Spirit) *who now holds it back will continue to do so till He is taken out of the way."* Now, think about every ruler in history that has caused chaos; put them all together, and you will not even come close to what the Bible says the Anti-Christ is going to be like. His reign of terror will bring anarchy on a worldwide scale.

Why in the world would I put these Scripture verses in this book? I did so for two reasons: **One**, these events will come to pass; we don't know when, but according to the prophecies about Christ returning in the air to gather His church that have been already fulfilled, this may happen sooner rather than later. **Two,** like He tells us about Hell, Jesus' return is described in the Bible to warn us that there will come a day when all that we know will change in an instant. So be ready for Christ's coming, and tell others to be ready, for on that day the world will be in chaos like it has never seen before.

The coming seven years of tribulation before Christ comes back to set up His kingdom here on earth is scary. Hell is scary. It may seem like I am trying to put fear into the hearts of whoever reads this book by writing about the Rapture, the Anti-Christ, and world chaos and suffering during what the Bible calls the seven years of tribulation. But how can anyone avoid such events if they don't know of their existence? The fear of judgement was the major factor for me in coming to Christ to have my sins forgiven. Now, I have no fear of Hell, but I am concerned about the events leading up to the seven years of tribulation. The world is changing very quickly to accommodate the coming of the Anti-Christ, and as this world changes, it's going to become harder to live the Christian life. But knowing about these coming events makes it easier to prepare for them. I also write about these things out of compassion for those who have yet to be reconciled with God. For God is not willing for any to perish, but for all to come to Him, to find Grace, and to have their fears replaced by His promises to take care of us through all circumstances. So if writing about these coming events helps someone see his or her need to accept Christ before the seven years of tribulation overwhelms the world, I think that person will be grateful to God for showing us in advance what is going to take place.

The Rapture

> *"Two men will be working together in the fields, and one will be taken, the other left. Two women will be going about their household tasks; one will be taken, the other left." – **Matthew 24:40–41***

These are not the easiest concepts to grasp, but they are part of Scripture. Remember, God has given you free will to believe whatever you want. But consider this: the prophecies written in the Bible have been 100% accurate thus far, and I don't think there is any reason to believe that the Bible prophecies concerning future events will be any different.

How should Bible prophecies on future events influence our lives? The prophecies that have already been fulfilled should give us a good foundation to believe in the prophecies that are yet to be fulfilled. This should be an encouragement to stand strong on the truths written in the Bible until Christ returns. If we disregard the teachings about future events, we will most certainly become overwhelmed when they are fulfilled, as in the days of Noah.

Noah and the Flood

Back in the days of Noah, the concept of a flood (when no one had ever seen rain) was a crazy idea to grasp. But for a stretch of 120 years while Noah built the ark, he prophesied that a flood was coming. His message of repentance was disregarded by all, and all perished.

Jesus uses the illustration of Noah in **Matthew 24:37–39:**

> *"As it was in the days of Noah, so it will be at the coming of the Son of Man (the rapture). For in the days before the flood, people were eating and drinking, marrying and giving in marriage, up to the day Noah entered the ark; and they knew nothing about what would happen until the flood came and took them all away. That is how it will be at the coming of (Jesus) the Son of Man."*

This is to warn us to take heed, and to not be like the people in Noah's time who disregarded Noah's preaching of future events concerning the flood.

The people of Noah's time became deaf to Noah's words about the coming flood, even though the ark was a huge sign that something was going to happen. Jesus makes this statement about their unbelief: *"they knew nothing about what would happen until the flood came and took them all away"* (**Matthew 24:39**). That statement can be summed up in two words—they were willfully **deaf** and **blind** by their own choosing. But is today's world responding any differently to the Bible's warnings of coming judgement?

Today, we have the same message to repent, but with one difference: we have the Holy Spirit to show us why we need to repent and believe in Jesus. It's not a flood we are trying to avoid, but as the Bible says, it's the coming judgement for a world that has turned its back on God.

I am sure some of you are thinking, "Mike, this the craziest thing I have ever heard." All I can say to that is: the rapture, the coming of the Anti-Christ, and the seven-year tribulation is written in the Bible as fact, not as abstract imagery. Only placing your faith in Christ will open your eyes to these hard passages of Scripture: *"Because they cannot see and understand the real meaning of the Scriptures. For this veil of misunderstanding can be removed only by believing in Christ"* (**2 Corinthians 3:14**).

Why are our eyes veiled? Because without a relationship with Christ, the Holy Spirit does not live inside us. The Holy Spirit works in the hearts of men to convict them of sinfulness, and if that sinfulness is dealt with by receiving Jesus Christ, the Holy Spirit comes to dwell within us, opening our eyes to the things of God.

"But we know about these things because God has sent his Spirit to tell us, and His Spirit searches out and shows us all of God's deepest secrets" **(1 Corinthians 2:10).** I will say it again: before I was saved, my eyes were veiled, making the Bible hard to read and understand. Now with the Holy Spirit dwelling within me, my eyes are open. Reading the Bible has become enjoyable, and as I allow the truth in Scripture to affect my heart, my relationship with Jesus grows more intimate and stronger.

18

ETERNAL SECURITY

Once you are saved, you are Heaven-bound.

*"All that the Father gives Me shall come to Me and the one who comes to Me I will certainly not cast out. For I have come down from heaven, not to do My own will, but the will of Him who sent Me. And this is the will of Him who sent Me, that of all that He has given Me I lose nothing, but raise it up on the last day. For this is the will of My Father, that everyone who beholds the Son and believes in Him, may have eternal life: and I Myself will raise him up on the last day." – **John 6:37–40***

In many verses in the Bible, God tells us that at the moment we receive the gift of salvation, our souls are entrusted into Jesus' hands for safekeeping, never to be lost again.

Again, one of my favourite verses on eternal security is **John 10:28–30:**

> *"And I give them eternal life, and they shall never perish; neither shall anyone snatch them out of My hand. My Father, who has given them to Me, is greater than all; and no one is able to snatch them out of My Father's hand. I and My Father are one."*

The Comfort of Eternal Security

In the fall of 1987, while sitting in church with my wife and eight-month-old son (our firstborn), a request came from the pulpit for anyone with mechanical experience to volunteer to travel to Haiti and repair a couple of diesel generators at a Mission Hospital in Cap-Haiten. Since I was a licensed mechanic with diesel experience, I turned to my wife and informed her that it was something I could do. That set in motion the preparation for a solo trip to Cap-Haiten a month later.

After all the preparations were made, I said goodbye to my wife and son at the Detroit Airport and flew to Miami, where I was to be picked up at my hotel room the next morning by the pilot who was to fly me to Haiti.

At the crack of dawn, the next day, the adventure continued when the pilot arrived at my hotel. He was just what you would picture an airplane captain would look like, wearing a white shirt with bars on the shoulders and a captain's hat. He was a tall man, probably at least 6'4" since the top of my head just came up to the top of his shoulders, and I'm 5'10" tall. He also had a persona about him that nothing could frazzle him or be out of his control.

I was able to get to know him a bit before the flight when we had breakfast together before heading to the airport. He was very pleasant and our conversation flowed with ease. When we arrived at the airport, he pulled up beside a big, old, grey Douglas DC-3 twin prop airplane that definitely had seen better days. He introduced me to John, the one and only ground crew member, then asked me if I would mind giving John a hand in getting the plane ready for our flight. As I looked at that old plane, I knew right away the comfort I experienced flying Delta was not going to be part of this flight.

I was glad to meet and learn a little bit about the captain before we took off; it boosted my confidence in flying in an old DC-3 airplane (that was probably built in the late thirties) in which I could see the ocean below through a quite large gap in the misaligned cargo doors as we flew.

A lot of prayer was offered on my behalf before I left for Haiti, which helped dispel some of the concerns I had about travelling to a country that was constantly in some sort of turmoil. But when arriving at the Mission Hospital in Cap-Haiten, I was still startled by the tall fences enclosing the hospital and the missionaries' living quarters.

Once there, I immediately settled into the task at hand, and after a week of working in heat to which I was not accustomed, I had both diesel generators working properly and producing electricity for the hospital. Having accomplished what I came to do, I was ready to go home.

On a very hot and sticky Friday morning, I boarded the same airplane that had brought me over from Miami, piloted by the same pilot. Squeezed in among boxes of cargo to be delivered to Port-au-Prince before we headed back to the States, I was glad to be on the first leg of my journey home. It was a quick flight from Cap-Haiten to Port-au-Prince airport. Once on the ground and taxied into position on the tarmac, the engines were shut down and I was ushered off the plane so it could be unloaded. I followed the captain a couple hundred feet to the airport complex where the front door had to be unlocked. I entered a waiting area that could easily hold one hundred people. I was instructed by the captain to take a chair and wait until he came back. Where could I go? I and the few people about twenty feet behind me were all locked in anyway—so I waited patiently.

After about an hour, the captain reappeared. The entrance door was then unlocked and left open for there was only me and a few other people left in the waiting area. As he walked towards me, he asked if I was ready to go. I just smiled and nodded my head yes. By this time, I was really missing my wife and baby and just wanted to get home. As the captain continued to walk over to the other group, I started out the door by myself towards the airplane. I didn't get more than thirty feet before a Haitian man dressed in military khaki clothing, carrying what seemed to be a WW2 sub-machine gun, came up to me looking very agitated. It didn't take long for me to figure out that I was the cause of his agitation when he began poking the barrel of his gun into my side.

Now, with my hands in the air, I just stood there, looking at him, wondering if this was the normal policy at the Port-au-Prince airport. The Haitian military guard was seemingly becoming more agitated with every question he asked me. I didn't have a clue what he was saying, but as he asked his questions, he would repeatedly poke me with the barrel of his gun. This still didn't help me understand a word he was staying, but plainly, he thought it might.

It wasn't until I saw the captain out of the corner of my eye almost running towards us with the other people from the waiting area in tow, that I felt something was really wrong. The captain was instantly engaged in a very passionate conversation with the Haitian guard—several times they looked at me, then back to the captain's clipboard, where I assume, the captain was trying to convince the guard that my name was on the roster sheet, and that I had just unintentionally walked onto the tarmac without realizing that I was supposed to wait for the captain's escort to the plane. After the heated discussion was over, the guard stopped pointing his gun at me and walked away.

At that moment, the captain turned to me, his teeth clenched, and his face marked with concern. He told me in a voice that you would use when you're out in public and wanted to get a child's attention without attracting attention to yourself, not to leave his side. As I looked up at him, a man I thought nothing could ever frazzle, I realized he was clearly frazzled. I agreed and then stuck to him like glue until I was strapped into my seat on the airplane.

On the flight back to Miami, as that old DC-3 bounced around in the sky while flying over the ocean, I looked out the window at the brilliant blue sky and reflected on what had just happened. I don't know how much danger I was in, or if things could have gotten so far out of control that my life could have ended right there on the tarmac, but one thing I did know: if things had gone badly, I would have been immediately in the presence of Jesus. That was a comfort I didn't possess when faced with my own mortality before I was saved by God's grace, five years prior.

Having the assurance that my eternal security is in God's hands, and not my own, is a great comfort, and a blessing for which I am thankful every day.

Can You Lose Your Salvation Once You Truly Accept Christ?

The answer is "no" because our salvation is in the power of God, not ourselves.

You may be like me: you might have made some wrong turns throughout your Christian walk and spent some time walking around in a desert of your own making. The feeling of being close to God had deserted you. But God will always work in our lives to bring us back into fellowship with Him. As I said before, "Love isn't a feeling; it's an act of the will." You fall out of love, then will yourself back into love. You fall out of fellowship with God—and you will yourself back into fellowship. You do this by first asking for forgiveness and then using repentance, a sincere regret, to change the direction of your life back to God.

Assurance of Eternal Life Is Bound in the Scriptures

When talking about God and Heaven, when asked, "Do you know for certain you're going to Heaven?" most people will answer, "Maybe," or "I don't know." That response confirms that people are trusting in themselves to get to Heaven. If they were trusting in Jesus, and only Jesus, to enter Heaven, they would know from **1 John 5:13,** which says, *"These things I have written to you who believe in the name of the Son of God, in order that you may know that you have eternal life,"* that they are Heaven-bound beyond a shadow of a doubt.

If I want a strong assurance of eternal life, I need to know what's in the Bible. I need to read it, study it, and meditate on it. Why? Because this is where **1 John 5:13** says the assurance of eternal life comes from: *"You may know that you have eternal life."*

Other benefits of knowing and reading your Bible are that it keeps you connected to Jesus and His promises, like the promise He gives of eternal life in **1 John 2:25,** which says, *"And this is what he* (Christ) *promised us—eternal life."* Also, by knowing God's Word and applying it to our lives, we will never be in danger of committing the unpardonable sin, as described in the next chapter.

19

THE UNPARDONABLE SIN

What Is It and Who Should Be Concerned?

The Billy Graham Evangelistic Association on the unpardonable sin: "Many Christians have heard that there is an unpardonable sin and live in dread that something grave they have done before or after conversion might be that sin. Their fears are unfounded. And while there is an unforgivable sin, it is not one that a true believer in Jesus Christ can commit. The one sin which God cannot forgive is mentioned in **Mark 3:28–30** and **Matthew 12:31–32**. Jesus had been performing miracles, including driving demons out of people by the power of the Holy Spirit. Instead of recognizing the source of Jesus' power and accepting Him as God's Son, the religious leaders accused Him of being possessed by the devil and driving demons out in the power of the devil. Jesus responded by saying, *"I tell you the truth, all the sins and blasphemies of men will be* *forgiven them. But whoever blasphemes against the Holy Spirit will never be forgiven; he is guilty of an eternal sin.* "xxii

The sin of the religious leaders—their blasphemy against the Holy Spirit—was a refusal to accept the witness of the Holy Spirit regarding who Jesus was and what He had come to do, and then submit their lives to Him. Jesus said concerning the Holy Spirit, *"When he* (the Holy Spirit) *comes, he will convict the world of guilt in regard to sin and righteousness and judgment"* **(John 16:8).** Anyone rejecting the conviction of their sin by the Holy Spirit will be in the same predicament as the religious leaders were in the days of Christ.

The point for us is that if we have received Jesus as our Saviour and Lord, we have not blasphemed or rejected the witness of the Holy Spirit concerning Christ; we have accepted His witness and believed.

The Bible explains that to commit the unpardonable sin, one must consciously, persistently, deliberately, and maliciously reject the testimony of the Spirit to the Deity and saving power of the Lord Jesus. If a person keeps doing that until death, there is no hope of forgiveness and eternal life in heaven.

Be careful: not all whose eyes are opened by the Holy Spirit acknowledge that their relationship with God is not right and that they should humble themselves and make that essential decision to receive Christ.

When the eyes are open — what's the risk in not making a decision immediately? As I said in my case, I was very aware that not making a decision was going to be considered rejection on my part, and I just knew that there might not be another opportunity. It was just too big of a risk to chance living in Hell for eternity. So, when the Holy Spirit convicted me of my sinfulness, I accepted Christ into my heart.

Unfortunately, I have seen a non-decision become a 'no' decision too many times. A heart being softened by the Holy Spirit, which sparks interest in talking about spiritual things, which could lead to conviction of sin and salvation, can be quenched very easily. For with the conviction of sin, it becomes evident there's a cost to saying yes to God. So those who have been drawn by the Holy Spirit can quickly grow cold when realizing the cost of following God would mean a change in lifestyle.

They want a relationship with God, and the security of knowing that they will go to Heaven, but still want to live the same life without change. This, God says, is impossible; coming to God, one needs to repent and change direction—becoming more like Christ, for that is the mark of a true believer. Some don't come out and just say "no" to God, but the conversations concerning God, sin, and salvation grow cold to the point of non-existence, never to be revisited again. For they feel living out the principles in **Luke 9:23** will just be too hard, so they hang onto their life as it is. *"Then he* (Jesus) *said to them all: 'Whoever wants to be my disciple must deny themselves and take up their cross daily and follow me.'"*

As I said before, when becoming a Christian, you want to become more like Christ, and that means giving up worldly things and denying the things of the flesh for the better things of God. That may sound like everything that is fun is out, but I can testify that is far from the truth. The transition to become like Christ is a lifetime undertaking that occurs as the Holy Spirit works in the heart of the believer. When the Holy Spirit changes the heart of the believer's wants and desires to align with what God wants for us, the transition does not take the fun out of life but increases its joy. I don't need any add-ons to have fun or enjoy myself like I did in the past. For in Christ, I now have peace and contentment, which if we were honest with ourselves, is the basic goal of life: having peace, contentment, and joy in all circumstances.

For many, the thought of leaving what is known is just too much. They know that their life isn't perfect, and down in their hearts they are feeling the call from the Holy Spirit to come to Christ, but they just can't make the transition. Too many variables, too many unknowns, and the comfort of familiarity is just too hard to break free of. Since the leap to God is just too unsettling, "maybe later" becomes the go-to response when future conversations about God and salvation come up. Unfortunately, many times, "maybe later" sadly turns into never, which grieves the Holy Spirit and becomes **the unpardonable sin.**

Two very different responses are possible when prompted by the Holy Spirit, and one of them could turn out to be the unpardonable sin. I have known two people who experienced a moving of the Holy Spirit in their hearts because of a book I asked them to read. It was the first book in the *Left Behind* series which talks about what it's going to be like when Christ comes back in what we call the Rapture to take those who have saving faith in Him up to Heaven before the final days on earth begin.

1 Thessalonians 4:16–17 presents a very clear picture of this event:

> *"For the Lord himself will come down from heaven, with a loud command, with the voice of the archangel and with the trumpet call of God, and the dead in Christ will rise first. After that, we who are still alive and are left will be caught up together with them in the clouds to meet the Lord in the air. And so we will be with the Lord forever."*

After this happens, those who are left behind will see a different world—a world where the righteousness of God is lifted from this earth. You think it's bad now, but let's just say that you don't want to be one of those left behind.

I know the two people to whom I recommended the *Left Behind* book quite well. Both had been involved in Bible-believing churches, knew about God and Christ, and lived, for the most part, a good moral life. They had head knowledge and could definitely use the right religious terms, but I wasn't so sure of where their hearts were towards God. After reading the book, both confided in me that if the Rapture really took place, they were quite sure they would be among those left behind. The Holy Spirit opened their eyes to the fact they weren't saved; their relationship with God wasn't in good standing.

When asked to receive Christ into his heart to receive forgiveness from God, one deliberately refused. He had been privileged by the Holy Spirit to learn the truth that his heart towards God wasn't right, but he was not ready to let go of worldly things. To this day, he still has not. If he doesn't repent before he dies, that will be the unpardonable sin.

The other made things right with God by accepting Jesus into his heart and receiving forgiveness. To this day, he is walking with God and becoming more like Christ, searching out the things of God through the Scriptures and applying them to his life.

Why did one heed the power of the Holy Spirit conviction of sin and accept Christ when the other didn't? One couldn't shake loose the pride of life which is, "I'll decide what's right and wrong. I'll run my own life. I'll sit on the throne of my heart. I'll make my own decisions. I'll do what I want to do. I'll go where I want to go. I'll be what I want to be." He completely rejected God's offer of forgiveness. The other humbled himself to God, giving up his pride, submitting to God's authority, and receiving God's forgiveness.

Pride never rears its ugly head so boldly as when it comes to accepting the Gospel of Jesus Christ. The outcome of **pride** ruling our decisions is to be **left behind.**

Jesus says this about being **left behind** in **Matthew 24:40– 44:**

> *"Two men will be in the field; one will be taken and the other left. Two women will be grinding with a hand mill; one will be taken and the other left. Therefore keep watch, because you do not know on what day your Lord will come."*

When Is Jesus Coming Back?

Jesus said in **Matthew 24:36,** *"But about that day or hour no one knows, not even the Angels in Heaven, not the Son, but only the Father."* This verse quoted by Jesus is strongly advising everyone to be ready for His coming at the time of the Rapture. That is where every believer in Christ will be transformed into their spiritual body and meet Him in the air to be with Him in Heaven. That may sound crazy on the surface, but for the believer, it's a promise that will come to pass, maybe sooner rather than later.

If your eyes are open only to what you can physically see, touch, and hear, God is never going to make sense to you, for Jesus says in **John 4:24,** *"God is spirit, and those who worship Him must worship in spirit and truth."*

At the front of the book, when I was sharing my testimony, I wrote this: "Looking back now, I understand that the answers to these questions and the choice to act upon them were the most important decisions I was ever going to make. It was also becoming quite clear that these decisions were more faith-based and involved something far beyond me. They were, in fact, far greater than something I could literally see, touch, and understand in my humanity." And that is exactly what I found; life and mortality have everything to do with the spiritual, and the spiritual has everything to do with God.

20

PAST SINS FORGOTTEN

After salvation, God chooses not to remember our past sins. *"Then he adds: 'Their sins and lawless acts I will remember no more. And where these have been forgiven, sacrifice for sin is no longer necessary'"* **(Hebrews 10:17–18).**

Earlier, I mentioned that all of our sins will be remembered by God. Every careless word we speak, we will have to give an account for.

In **Hebrews 10:17** it's said that *"Their sins and lawless acts I will remember no more."* This verse is not a contradiction; it's a declaration for those who have accepted Christ and have become children of God.

John 1:12 says:

> *"Yet to all who did receive him (Christ), to those who believed in his name (Christ), he gave the right to become children of God."*

Those who believe in Christ's name will not be judged for past, present, or future sins; the price has been paid and the slate has been wiped clean. What a wonderful concept; as **Micah 7:19** puts it, our sins *"will be thrown into the depths of the sea."*

Forgiveness Without Punishment

When I was first saved, I had such issues with this concept. I just could not believe that God could choose not to remember heinous crimes that people had committed just because they came to the cross and asked for forgiveness. It just seemed too easy. I had no problem forgiving and not punishing those who had committed small infractions. But what about a ruthless murderer? What about a person who shows brutality or those who are caught up in the evil depravities of mankind? How can all those acts just be forgiven and forgotten?

- Where is the justice in that?
- Where is the justice for the victims?
- Shouldn't God punish them first, before they are worthy of forgiveness?
- Those who have done such things, should they even be allowed to be forgiven?

So why did I have such a problem with how God freely gave out His forgiveness? Because my view of sin wasn't right. I gauged my sin in comparison to those who were worse sinners than me. My hypothesis was, I had never murdered anyone physically, so I was in better standing with God than the murderer. Since this thinking made me morally superior to most of society in my mind, I was okay to receive God's forgiveness.

Let's not bring up the fact that Jesus warns us that if we have hatred in our heart towards someone, we have already committed murder, along with every other sin there is. If it's in your heart, you're already guilty of it. I wasn't seeing my sins from the perspective of a Holy God. I wasn't seeing how heinous my sins were in His sight. I wasn't seeing that my sins were an act totally against His righteousness.

Because of my newness of faith, I just didn't know enough about how God's grace and righteousness worked hand in hand. Who can fully understand the depth of His unmerited grace? I know I can't. But I am glad that it was imparted to me. And as I came to understand the things of God better, I saw my sins for what they were in His sight: acts totally against Him. In fact, if my sins were totally against Him, then that gives Him the right to forgive those sins. Over the years, I have come to realize that there is no disclaimer on which sins can be forgiven. All sins can be forgiven. I appreciate God's grace for what it is; unmerited forgiveness for all who come humbly to the cross and ask for it with no exceptions.

If you think there should actually be some criteria to be met before coming to God, then the question is who determines that criteria? We can't know a man's heart like God does, so what man would be able to judge who is worthy of forgiveness or not? Could I step in and set the degree of sins that could be forgiven? Could you? Could we even start to come up with, and administer, a degree of punishment so that one could become worthy to repent and seek forgiveness? **No,** for that's not how God's grace works. No one has to jump through hoops to come to Christ. If the Holy Spirit opens someone's heart to Jesus, that is all that is needed.

In **John 8:7** and **8:9–11** the religious leaders brought a woman to Jesus who was caught in the act of adultery. The religious leaders explained to Jesus the Law of Moses, saying that it required her to be stoned to death. They were trying to trap Jesus by His own teaching on forgiveness.

Jesus Shows Forgiveness without Shame

> *"When they kept on questioning Him, He straightened up and said to them, 'Let any one of you who is without sin be the first to throw a stone at her.'"* – **John 8:7**

> *"At this, those who heard began to go away one at a time, the older ones first, until only Jesus was left, with the woman still standing there. Jesus straighten up and asked her, 'Woman, where are they? Has no one condemned you?' 'No one, sir' 'Then neither do I condemn you,' Jesus declared. 'Go now and leave your life of sin.'"* – **John 8:9–11**

Jesus offered the opportunity for anyone in the crowd to administer punishment—*"you who is without sin be the first to throw a stone at her"*— but there were no takers; no one there was without sin other than Jesus. So, only those without sin can have a problem with God forgetting past sins and imparting grace to those they don't think deserve it because of their reprehensible sins. Since no one is sinless, we sinners must trust in God's righteous administration of His grace to all who will receive it.

One very important thing Jesus said to the woman was that He didn't condemn her, and to leave her sinful life behind. He didn't say go beat yourself up for a while then come back, and we'll talk. He simply said, *"Go now and leave your life of sin."*

Just remember, though, that you can't have it both ways: After receiving Jesus' forgiveness, and as the Holy Spirit works in your life, there will be a change of heart toward sin. Leaving your life of sin for the better things of God is living proof that Jesus has taken up residence in your heart. But if you ask for Jesus' forgiveness to escape judgement without changing your view of sin, don't think your hollow words fooled God; He sees the intentions of the heart, and no one is ever going to fool Him.

> *"The Lord does not look at the things people look at. People look at the outward appearance, but the Lord looks at the heart." – 1 Samuel 16:7*

Note: When God looks at our hearts, He is really looking at our actions, which divulge what's really in our hearts.

Remember that there is no forgiveness without punishment. Someone will take the punishment for every sin committed by man. The question is, are you going to let Jesus step in and take your punishment? Or are you going to receive the just reward for your own sin on judgement day, which is eternity in Hell.

If you allow Jesus to step in and take your punishment, you will be forgiven for your past, present, and future sins. Past sins won't be easy to erase from your memory, just as present and future sins won't be easy to make amends for or forget. No, the only one who won't remember is God. We will live with the consequences of our actions, and those consequences don't disappear just because we are forgiven. The sign of a true believer is repenting of our sin, which means turning from it. *"Go now and leave your life of sin"* **(John 8:11),** making amends if possible, and living and growing to be more and more like Christ on a daily basis. As we grow to be more like Christ, we will sin less, but we will never be perfect until we get to Heaven. That's why we need to confess our daily sins to Jesus, for He says in **1 John 1:9,** *"If we confess our sins, He is faithful and just and will forgive us our sins and purify us from all unrighteousness."*

Remembering Past Sins

You might be wondering how to deal with past sins that still haunt you, even though God has forgiven you.

Remember what **Vince Vitale** said: "I can look back at my life as a teenager right now and say I thought at that time some of the things I did were no big deal, but the reality is they were truly terrible."[xxiii]

So, what can we do? Regretting what we have done before being saved is a sign that we are saved. Pray for those we hurt in the past, for there is really no excuse for inappropriate behaviour in the first place. Humbly ask for God's forgiveness for each specific offense, repent, and stop committing those sins. Then take comfort that God's forgiveness can release us from the shame and guilt that we carry. We can't go back and change one thing from our past. And in many cases, we can't even go back and find the people we've hurt over the years and ask them to forgive us.

But remembering those people we've hurt to God in prayer does help—first, in forgiving ourselves, and second, through God's ability to bring healing into their lives through our prayers. We should not let regret overwhelm us, but we do need to remember how our past sins have hurt others and let that spur us on to become more like Christ in all avenues of our lives. *"Whoever says he abides in Him* (Jesus) *ought to walk in the same way in which he* (Jesus) *walked"* **(1 John 2:6).**

What about Our Present Sins?

Even though we have been forgiven, we still sin, and usually on a daily basis. Jesus gives us an example of how we should pray and ask for forgiveness in **Matthew 6:9–15:**

> *"This, then, is how you should pray: 'Our Father in Heaven, hallowed be your name, your kingdom come, your will be done, on earth as it is in Heaven. Give us today our daily bread. And forgive us our debts, as we also have forgiven our debtors. And lead us not into temptation but deliver us from the evil one. For if you forgive other people when they sin against you, your heavenly Father will also forgive you. But if you do not forgive others their sins, your Father will not forgive your sins.'"*

The Lord's Prayer talks about asking for and giving daily forgiveness. It also asks God to forgive our daily sins (debts), and to grant forgiveness to anyone that sins against us. This action is not adding to God's initial act of forgiveness (reconciliation) that we experienced when we first believed in Jesus. This action is the process of becoming more like Christ in the way of forgiving anyone that has sinned against us. If we are stubborn in forgiving those who have sinned against us, God is not going to forgive us, plain and simple. Not forgiving others puts us in the position of willfully sinning against Him, and *"Jesus declared, 'Go now and leave your life of sin'"* **(John 8:11).**

As we find it in our hearts to forgive others, we also have to find it in our hearts to accept God's forgiveness for former sins over which we keep beating ourselves up. Jesus wants us to forgive ourselves after we have confessed those sins to Him. Once He forgives us of our sin, He remembers them no more. So, after we have confessed our sins and made amends, we need to let them go as well.

Rehashing our sins and hanging onto guilty feelings is not helpful. Jesus died on the cross for all of our sins—not some, but all. So, forgiveness in Him is complete. Stop believing the devil's lies that we are still guilty; rather, stand on God's Word and trust in His grace completely. I think the hardest person in my life to apply God's daily forgiveness to is me, but God commands that I do so.

> "Remembering our sins is only beneficial when it reminds us of the extent of God's forgiveness, which should make it easier for us to forgive others" **(Matthew 18:21–35)** (gotquestions.org).[xxiv]

God Gives a Promise: If you're having a hard time letting go of confessed sin, which is still harassing you, and can't find peace of mind, follow the Apostle Paul's instructions.

In Philippians 4:8–9

"Finally, brothers and sisters, whatever is true, whatever is noble, whatever is right, whatever is pure, whatever is lovely, whatever is admirable—if anything is excellent or praiseworthy—think about such things. Whatever you have learned or received or heard in me (The Apostle Paul), or seen in me—put it into practice. And the God of peace will be with you."

When I fill my mind with everything in these verses, sinning isn't a problem, depression isn't a problem, and anxiety is nowhere to be found—for the promise God gives in this Scripture is, in Him—peace will be with you.

Daily Forgiveness

We ask God for daily forgiveness because we are still going to sin on this side of Heaven. We are not going to be perfect until we walk through Heaven's gates, so to both offer forgiveness to others and to accept it from God as we live our lives is a necessity for any Christian to have close fellowship with God.

"What the Apostle John is referring to in **1 John 1:8–10**, which says, *'If we claim to be without sin, we deceive ourselves and the truth is not in us. If we confess our sins, he is faithful and just and will forgive us our sins and purify us from all* *unrighteousness. If we claim we have not sinned, we make him out to be a liar and his word is not in us...'* is the day-to-day cleansing we obtain when we confess our sins in order to restore fellowship with our heavenly Father—the fellowship which is interrupted by the daily tarnishing of sin that affects us all. This is not the all-inclusive cleansing from sin that comes with salvation by grace through faith but is more like the foot-washing Jesus describes in **John 13:10**. The *'whole body is clean,'* He told the disciples, but their feet were dirty from their walking in the world (gotquestions.org)."[xxv]

21

LIVING FOR CHRIST

Life as a Believer Is a Progression

After accepting Christ, it's all about living in Christ, thinking how He thinks, acting how He would act, and showing the kind of mercy and compassion that He would show. It's that simple, but I won't try to fool you; it's hard to do. Why? Because as I mentioned before, our old nature doesn't want to stay dead.

Here is a simplistic example of starting a walk with Christ. You go to the gym or try to lose weight by eating better, and your body fights you every step of the way. I know this from personal experience over the years. But when going to the gym becomes a way of life, it becomes enjoyable and benefits us. When eating right becomes part of our daily diet, again, it's good for us and not a burden. It's the same with our new walk with Christ: when it becomes part of who we are, it's not a burden.

"When someone becomes a Christian, he or she becomes a brand new person inside. They are not the same anymore, a new life has begun!" – 2 **Corinthians 5:17**

This new life is a progression. We grow into maturity, for if God had brought to mind all the things I needed to work on all at once, I would have just given up. Christ didn't save me to cast me down with guilt and shame; just the opposite, in fact. He took away my guilt and shame.

He says in **Matthew 11:28–30:**

"Come to me, all you who are weary and burdened, and I will give you rest. Take my yoke upon you and learn from me, for I am gentle and humble in heart, and you will find rest for your souls. For my yoke is easy and my burden is light."

Jesus takes away all of the spiritual burdens of trying to work our way to Heaven. The yoke to which Jesus is referring is a frame of wood by which two oxen are joined at the neck, thus enabling them to pull together. A younger ox would be put together with an older, more experienced ox to teach the younger to pull alongside and share the work. At first, the older ox is doing the work, pulling the young ox along, teaching him to relax, to not fight against the yoke, and to pull in harmony and work together. As the younger ox learns not to fight against the yoke, his burden becomes lighter, and his focus is unswerving, straight, and even agreeable.

The example of the yoke isn't about our physical burdens, but our spiritual burdens.

A quote from gotquestions.org on **Matthew 11:28–30** gives a good perspective on what Jesus meant.

"Jesus was saying that any kind of law-keeping is burdensome and amounts to a 'heavy yoke' of oppression because no amount of law-keeping can bridge the gap between our sinfulness and God's holiness. God says, through the mouth of the prophet Isaiah, that all of our righteous deeds are like 'dirty rags,' and Paul reiterated in Romans that, *no one will be declared righteous in his sight by observing the law'* **(Romans 3:20).** The good news is that Jesus promises to all who come to Him that He will give them rest from the heavy burden of trying to earn our way into Heaven and rest from the oppressive yoke of self-righteousness and legalism. Jesus encourages those who are 'heavy laden' to take His yoke upon them, and in doing so, they will find rest for their souls. The yoke of Jesus is light and easy to carry because it is the yoke of repentance and faith, followed by a singular commitment to follow Him. As the apostle John says, *'For this is the love of God, that we keep his commandments. And his commandments are not burdensome'* **(1 John 5:3).** What makes Jesus' yoke easy and His burden light is that in Jesus' own active obedience (i.e., His perfect fulfillment of the Law of God), He carried the burden that we were meant to carry. His perfect obedience is applied (imputed) to us through faith, just as His righteousness was exchanged for our sin at the cross **(2 Corinthians 5:21).** Our obedience to Jesus then becomes our 'spiritual worship' **(Romans 12:1).** Furthermore, we are in-dwelt by the Holy Spirit who works in our lives to mold us into the image of Christ, thereby making the yoke of Jesus easy and His burden light. The life lived by faith is a much lighter yoke and a much easier burden to carry than the heavy and burdensome yoke of self-righteousness under which some continually strive to make themselves acceptable to God through works."[xxvi]

Why does the Bible talk so much about the foolhardiness of striving to find God's favour with our works? Because the root of that reasoning is pride. To recap on man's pride, "I'll decide what's right and wrong. I'll run my own life. I'll sit on the throne of my heart. I'll make my own decisions. I'll do what I want to do. I'll go where I want to go. I'll be what I want to be."

One consistent factor with all man-based religions is works; the idea that man has to work hard to earn God's favour is just one example. Another aspect of man-based religions is fear, making God out to be terrifying and untouchable, only approachable through the higher hierarchy of the church. This higher hierarchy modifies the behaviour of its followers by fear, guilt, and shame for their own benefit. Even some so-called Christian denominations try to add works to God's grace, which

God finds unpardonable. He makes it absolutely clear in **Ephesians 2:8–9:**

> *"For it is by grace that you have been saved, through faith and this not from yourselves: it is the gift of God: not by works, so that no one can boast."*

I have used this Scripture quotation a few times now because of its clarity. It shows that we will be saved by grace, and not by works, fear, guilt, or shame. Salvation is a gift, and what kind of gift would have any of those negative qualities?

When Christ says in **John 15:5,** *"He who abides in Me, and I in him bears much fruit; for without Me you can do nothing,"* He doesn't seem to characterize anything but love for those with whom He wants to have fellowship. In **Romans 8:38–39,** The Apostle Paul wrote that nothing is ever going to separate us from God's love:

> *"For I am convinced that neither death nor life, neither angels nor demons, neither the present nor the future, nor any powers, neither height nor depth, nor anything else in all creation, will be able to separate us from the love of God that is in Christ Jesus our Lord."*

Amazingly, the gift of God's love through Jesus Christ comes with a big promise attached—it can't be broken, and it's for eternity.

The Progression Continues: Changing the Way We View Our Lives

"Therefore, if anyone is in Christ, the new creation has come: The old has gone, the new is here!" – **1 Corinthians 5:17**

If the new is **'here,'** I needed to make some changes in the **'here'** now. The best example I can give is when I was having a special guest over to my house for dinner for the first time. My four kids and I had been living in our house for many years. Life was very busy with work, and the responsibilities of raising four kids alone and getting them to their extracurricular activities did not leave a lot of time for deep cleaning. To us, the house looked great; it had a kind of lived-in look—well, a very lived-in look. Before our special guest arrived, and before we started cleaning, I asked everyone to look around and try to envision the house as the person who was coming for dinner would see it. I noted that our guest's home didn't have any extra clutter. When we started to look at the house through someone else's eyes, we saw it in a totally different light; it wasn't as clean as we thought because we had grown accustomed to the clutter, the dust bunnies, some spider webs in the corners, and the general untidiness.

This is what it's like when Christ comes into our hearts. The Holy Spirit puts a spotlight on the areas of our lives that need to be cleaned. We start to see the clutter of sin, the dust bunnies of poor behaviour, the spider webs of offense, and the general untidiness of living without Christ in our lives. Now, looking at our lives through the eyes of Christ, we should actively start cleaning house, getting rid of the old and bringing in the new.

> *"That, however, is not the way of life you learned when you heard about Christ and were taught in him in accordance with the truth that is in Jesus. You were taught, with regard to your former way of life, to put off your old self, which is being corrupted by its deceitful desires; to be made new in the attitude of your minds; and to put on the new self, created to be like God in true righteousness and holiness."* – **Ephesians 4:20–24**

Becoming more like Christ: As Billy Graham puts it, "Being a Christian is more than just an instantaneous conversion. It is a daily process whereby you grow to be more and more like Christ."[xxvii]

When you begin, you start out as a babe. You must be fed on the simple things of the Bible. As you learn to walk in your Christian life, you will fall and make mistakes at times, but that's okay. God uses those times to teach—resulting in maturity.

We are forgiven, but as I mentioned before, we won't be sinless until we pass through Heaven's gates. If God, through the Holy Spirit, is going to continue to make us more like Christ, we have to work at getting rid of our old selves and bad habits. Thank God it's a progression instead of being all at once. The start of that progression occurs when we start to integrate the instructions in **Colossians 3:7–9** into our lives:

"You used to walk in these ways, in the life you once lived. But now you must also rid yourselves of all such things as these: anger, rage, malice, slander, and filthy language from your lips. Do not lie to each other, since you have taken off your old self with its practices."

God doesn't expect the new believer who is just beginning to study and learn His Word and precepts to understand the whole scope of their sinfulness or to have the same understanding of God's holiness as a mature believer. But growth brings understanding, which brings maturity; and that is what God asks of us when we become a Christian.

We may not have a problem with all the sins that are listed in **Colossians 3:7–9,** but there are probably a few that bother us. We work on what the Holy Spirit convicts us of first, and then move on to the next. We may have to revisit some a few times over the years, but as we do the work, we will definitely see our lives as an ongoing progression, conforming to the image of Christ.

As the Bible says, salvation is a one-time decision, but the Christian life is a progression from being a babe in Christ into a mature person in Christ.

How God Interacts with the New Believer

If a toddler throws a temper tantrum while sitting in his highchair and throws his milk onto the floor, we wouldn't treat him the same way we would correct a teenager who had done the same at the supper table. God does not correct new Christians like He would a mature Christian either. A new Christian is referred to as a babe in Christ and is nurtured along accordingly. Our Heavenly Father will never correct us using guilt and shame. He works just the opposite. He corrects with a love and patience that we can barely comprehend this side of Heaven.

God works in our lives through the Holy Spirit to bring us to maturity and changes us in the sequence where it's most needed. Some changes are easy to spot. In my life, I was first convicted of swearing and using the Lord's name in vain. While the conviction came quickly, it was hard to change. Thirty-seven years ago, if I screwed up and swore, I would feel bad and try to do better. Today, if I swear, I am heartbroken not only that a word like that slipped out of my mouth, but also that I thought it up in my heart in the first place. The difference between then and now is that I have a different view of sin. I know now that Christ paid a heavy price for my sin on the cross. I don't like grieving Him when I know I can act better.

At the start of my Christian life, I was mostly working on my outward appearance; for example, swearing, drinking, and being in places that I knew I shouldn't be. I didn't look like a good Christian most of the time. My life personified the phrase, "But for God's grace, there go I." The saying means that I am not perfect, but because of God's Grace, I am perfect in His eyes, but still a work in progress here on earth.

The sins I am working on now in my life are very different compared to the sins that I was working on when I first got saved. One thing I am working on now is harmful attitudes. These attitudes have been in my family for generations and need to be broken so that they are not continually handed down to future generations. These are attitudes of arrogance and conceit, to name a few, which always lead to harshness and anger. These types of attitudes have done nothing but cause hurt and pain in my life, mainly with relationships. Your generational sins may not be the same as mine, but if you look hard enough, you're going to find some.

Change is usually hard, but changing to be better seems to be really hard. So many things can hold us back from walking close to Christ, but I know when my relationship with Christ is right, the sins of arrogance and conceit are much easier to keep in check. I need to keep my walk with Christ strong for the simple reason that it makes my relationships with others, and especially with my wife and grown children, so much healthier.

22

FREE WILL

The Old Nature: Our Stumbling Block

In the early eighties, I entered into a relationship with Jesus Christ. It hasn't always been easy, as over the years I have continually struggled with getting control over my prideful nature that says, "I'll decide what's right and wrong. I'll run my own life. I'll sit on the throne of my heart. I'll make my own decisions. I'll do what I want to do. I'll go where I want to go. I'll be what I want to be."

I still have free will to choose how I want to live my life, even if it grieves the Holy Spirit and Christ Himself.

But as **Vince Vitale** says: "Jesus invites us into a relationship with Himself, noting a relationship can only be entered into if both people say yes to that relationship. If we're not willing to say yes to that relationship, then Jesus can do nothing on His side."[xxviii]

Furthermore, being in a relationship with Jesus does not mean that He will overpower our free will. We still choose the intensity of our relationship, for He doesn't want puppets on a string. The greatest gift we can give back to Jesus is willingly following Him with our whole heart, soul, and mind. But following Jesus with all my heart, soul, and mind is often in stark contrast to what my free will wants. My free will can be very stubborn, even opposing the good things God has for me. At those times, I can say my free will is my downfall, or my nemesis.

Emphasizing our free will to decide, consider this quote from A.W. Tozer: "It may be said without qualification that every man is as holy and as full of the Spirit as he wants to be. He may not be as full as he wishes he were, but he is most certainly as full as he wants to be."[xxix] Our relationship with Jesus Christ is always influenced by our free will: either to make it stronger or weaker.

Pridefulness Always Equals Poor Choices

Unfortunately, some years after I accepted Jesus, I got away from living victoriously. As a result of pride, poor decisions took Christ from the proper place in my heart, which He deserved; and I substituted my own wants and desires. This removed His vital influence on the way I was living. Even though I started to live a half-hearted Christian life, God still did not violate my free will. Apostle Paul in Romans talks about my dilemma:

> *"So you see how it is: my new life tells me to do right, but the old nature that is still inside me loves to sin. Oh, what a terrible predicament I'm in!*

Who will free me from my slavery to this deadly lower nature? Thank God! It has been done by Jesus Christ our Lord. He has set me free." – **Romans 7:25**

Yes, the Lord had set me free from my sinful life, but for reasons I will talk about later, I put myself back into the bondage of sin.

The Old Nature

The old nature is the biggest con artist there is, and he lives in each one of us. A con artist is defined as a person who cheats or tricks others by persuading them to believe something that is not true. That's why the Bible is clear on what to do with the **old nature** after we accept Christ:

"For we know that our old self (or old nature) was crucified with Him (Christ) so that the body ruled by sin might be done away with, that we should no longer be slaves to sin — because anyone who has died (killed that old self) has been set free from sin." – **Romans 6:6–7**

One time when things in my life were not going so well and I was feeling very vulnerable, the con artist in me, my old nature, convinced me that my old life of sin would comfort me more than trusting in God. Believing this lie was clearly not a good idea, and I knew deep down that there would be consequences. Still, I blatantly disregarded the Holy Spirit's prompting to stop and turn to God for help. I exercised my free will and gave in to my old nature, handing that old con artist control of my life, putting myself back into the bondage of sin from which I had worked so hard to be free. I was willfully giving up my freedom and letting sin once again rule my life. Looking back, I realized what a fool I had been.

I was still a child of God, though, and **John 10:28–29** was still true:

> *"I give them eternal life, and they shall never perish; no one will snatch them out of my hand. My Father, who has given them to me, is greater than all; no one can snatch them out of my Father's hand."*

But returning to my sinful life had put distance between Christ and me; the close fellowship was severed because I had grieved Him. Jesus never pulled away from me, but He also didn't force the relationship. And because of His perfect love, He was always mindful of my free will to choose the level of intimacy in our relationship. When my irresponsible behaviour fractured our relationship, He still didn't force me to obey. If love is forced, it's not love, but obligation.

When I gave my heart to Jesus in the early eighties, three things happened concerning the Holy Spirit. First, He came to reside in my heart and now guides me in the ways of righteousness—helping me become more like Christ. Second, the Holy Spirit takes my prayers to the Father on my behalf. Third, the Holy Spirit makes known to me any sin that needs to be confessed and forsaken. The Holy Spirit, being God, is mindful of my free will, but does put the pressure on me to take heed, repent, and come back into fellowship.

Another thing that happened when I received Christ was that I became a child of God; and like any good parent, Jesus put the pressure on me to come back into fellowship. He knew that outside of Him, I was heading for trouble. When I started making decisions that pulled me away, that's exactly what happened. I had to walk in the desert of my own making for a while, but God never left me, nor did He give up on me.

Jesus' Arms Are Always Open

Jesus never stopped using the Holy Spirit to convict me of my waywardness. He needed to open my eyes to why I had drifted away and to soften my heart so I would deal with what had led me astray in the first place. Jesus never made it hard for me to come back; His arms were always open. And it was so simple— all I had to do was ask. After years of doing things my way and making decisions that I thought were going to make me happy but didn't, I did exactly that. I asked for forgiveness, repented (changed how I was living), and came back home.

Reconciling my relationship with Christ is no different than hurting a good friend, then realizing your mistake and asking for forgiveness. The friendship may be a little tense for a while, but after amends are made and forgiveness is given, healing will occur. In my case, I knew if I didn't deal with what had caused me to stray in the first place, I really wasn't serious about repenting; and without repentance, one can't be granted forgiveness. When I finally did deal with my past (which I will talk about in the following pages), the good news is that Jesus, who is always faithful to forgive and restore the relationship, did exactly that, with pure forgiveness and no residual hurt attached.

To obtain forgiveness, we simply follow the admonition of **1 John 1:9:** *"If we confess our sins, he is faithful and just and will forgive us our sins and purify us from all unrighteousness."*

The restoration of the relationship is not the same as the one-time forgiveness of sin that Christ paid for on the cross. For example, if one of my kids does something wrong, that child doesn't stop being my child. Nothing can change that relationship, no matter what my child does. Depending on what my kid does, I might sometimes hope others don't know he's my child, if for no other reason than to curb my embarrassment. But my child simply needs to ask for forgiveness and repent—stop doing wrong—to restore our relationship.

It is the same with God. If we become unfaithful in our walk with Him, we just need to confess and repent to restore our relationship. Nothing else needs to be done; there's no prescribed time of guilt and shame. We don't lose the gift of salvation, and we don't stop being a child of God. If we confess and ask for forgiveness, God forgives and forgets. In this world, we will continue to sin, and asking for forgiveness is a process we will do many times through our Christian lives with God and others. We are just not going to be perfect this side of Heaven.

Why Did I Get Off Track?

One reason might have been because we added works to grace, which never works. I have always been very performance oriented. I was going to be the best Christian ever, the only problem was that I started to use the old, faithful Ten

Commandments as my performance yardstick: the do's and don'ts; that's what it came down to. I went to church three times a week, worked in the bus ministry, got rid of my TV, and went door-to-door witnessing to share the Gospel. But at some point, my motivation became prideful, and that's when I stopped serving the Lord for the joy of His gift of salvation and did it out of feelings of obligation. I had lost the joy of serving God with a humble heart. I was working hard for self and looking for adulation from my fellow Christians. I had put on, once again, the heavy yoke of trying to please God by works. My spiritual walk had become legalism (an adherence to moral law rather than to personal faith or stressing obedience apart from faith), and it was showing in my irritability and anger at life in general. I was performing out of a guilty conscience, and I became apathetic.

My relationship with Christ had become strained because I became the very thing He talked against to the religious leaders when He was on earth. I was showboating and doing things to be seen by my fellow man. All Jesus asked of me was to be in a relationship with Him and to become more like Him, but I made my Christian faith into a competition because I never got rid of that Ten Commandments mentality.

In reality, I don't need any commandments to tell me what is right or wrong. I know right away if I have done or said something that isn't proper or that is hurtful to someone; that is still true to this day. I know straight away if I am gossiping because a little voice (my God-given conscience) in my head tells me it's not right and to stop.

I have had times when I was convicted in my heart to make something right but ignored the prompting of my conscience. I just put it out of my mind, only to have the Holy Spirit convict me again of these wrongs and prompt me to go make amends, even years later. After I obeyed, I felt as if a weight had been lifted off me. We know what is right and wrong in our hearts—God made us that way—and trying to cover up unconfessed sin is foolish, for we know it's never going to lie dormant. We hear on the news about someone brought to justice years after a crime. Some say they were glad they were finally caught because it was tormenting them every day. The scary ones are the ones whose conscience is completely seared. In those, evil abounds.

The Restless Tongue

I also don't need any commandments to understand how poorly I control my own tongue, even when the little voice in my head keeps saying, "Shut up, Mike."

> *"But no human being can tame the tongue. It is a restless evil, full of deadly poison. With the tongue we praise our Lord and Father, and with it we curse human beings, who have been made in God's likeness. Out of the same mouth come praise and cursing. My brothers and sisters, this should not be."* – **James 3:8–10**

If I were to write out all of the misspoken words, hurtful comments, and dumb statements I have said over my lifetime, there wouldn't be a book big enough to hold all of those pages. I cringe at some of the things that have come out of my mouth when I was trying to be cool, or be sarcastic, or mask my insecurities. All I know is, if nothing else, my tongue alone defeats me.

This is why it has to be all God's grace; I just can't reach God's standards of righteousness on my own. My tongue and sinful thoughts simply prove that on a daily basis.

Thankfully, even though I am a defeated man in my own strength, with God's strength, I am useable to Him.

> *"I can do all things through Christ who strengthens me." –* **Philippians 4:13**

Asking Forgiveness for a Restless Tongue

Since I have a hard time controlling my tongue at times, I have had to make amends and ask for forgiveness many times over. This is not pleasant for me, as admitting that I am wrong and humbly asking for forgiveness is my least favourite thing to do. Like I said, I am always dealing with my pride. The silver lining is, it does motivate me to think before I speak. So, if you're one of the ones I have offended with my speech, and I wasn't astute enough to figure it out in time to apologize—I'm sorry. I am so glad that I am not going to have the problem of saying the wrong things anymore when I get to Heaven.

23

OVERCOMING PERSONAL ISSUES

The Bible tells me I am a new creature in Christ. So how did I lose sight of Christ and resort to old ways and habits? In addition to my tongue, my other problem was that I hadn't dealt with my personal issues from growing up. I was always running away from my past hurts, both the ones done to me and those done to others. This prevented me from fully accepting all of Christ's forgiveness that I so desperately needed. Overall, I felt forgiven for the fact that I was born into sin, which Christ paid for on the cross. I knew I was Heaven-bound when I died, but I did not really feel totally forgiven for all of the personal mistakes I had made throughout my life. Those mistakes were locked away in the dark rooms of my heart. But God wasn't satisfied with just some of the rooms of my life being cleaned, for He could see what effect those rooms of darkness were having on my life; and He wanted them cleaned once and for all. I kept those rooms locked up tight, for I didn't know how to deal with some of the sins from my youth that were outside of my control.

As I look back at those youthful mistakes through the eyes of a mature adult, I am still haunted by these questions: Why didn't I run? Why did I let myself be manipulated? Why didn't I have courage to stand? These troubling questions always caused me to beat myself up even though my circumstances at that age were out of my control. This led me to ask the questions somewhat bitterly to God: Where was He in my time of need? If He was such a loving God, why didn't He protect me?

That kind of thinking was asking God to do something out of His character: to take away my free will and the free will of everyone else who was involved so that I wouldn't have been hurt. The past can't be rewritten, but dealing with the past properly is the only way to have a worthwhile future. One thing I am very glad for is that, though I went through a lot of pain and disappointment, I never blamed or was bitter towards God to the point of never having anything to do with Him. By abandoning God, I would have lost out on the most important relationship of my life: my relationship with Jesus Christ. Jesus gives me a hope and a future in Him, through which I have been able to forgive and move on.

Unfortunately, this is something that I see many people who are hurt and in pain not do—be able to forgive and move on. They blame God, holding bitterness in their hearts, and turn from the only one who could bring total healing to their broken and bitter heart.

God Doesn't Hurt People, But We Do

We inflict emotional and physical pain on one another because of our sinful nature. Then we take that emotional and physical pain, and instead of dealing with it, we internalize it and proceed to wallow in it for years to come. That's what I did. I internalized all those hurts and watched the outcome ruin my life. Even though I was a Christian, I didn't bring these issues to God wholeheartedly. And since God is never too keen on half-heartedness, that didn't work out.

As a result, I returned to the things of the world to find comfort, and this path brought me only more pain and a greater feeling of loneliness. When I was lost and at the end of my rope, I was so grateful God provided a miracle in my life. It would have been nice if it was all at once, but it took years. Because of my free will, I still had the last say on how long this process was going to take. And most of the time, I am my own worst enemy.

It wasn't until the year 2000, when I lost my job of 23 years and my wife left me, that my situation truly started to change. I had to face the fact that everything Michael Borthwick was, or thought he was, demolished—gone. Oddly enough, I was right where God needed me to be to start the inner healing that I so desperately needed but had never wholeheartedly sought.

Looking back now, I am so glad God didn't give up on me. **Philippians 1:3–6** says:

> *"I thank my God every time I remember you. In all my prayers for all of you, I always pray with joy because of your partnership in the gospel from the first day until now, being confident of this, that*

he who began a good work in you will carry it on
to completion until the day of Christ Jesus."

And in **Hebrews 13:5,** God says, *"Never will I leave you;*
never will I forsake you," and God never did; but He worked in
my life year after year to bring me to the point of obtaining
healing.

Even though I was at the very end of myself, I was still not
quite ready to surrender all to God. I was holding back from Him
the painful areas that I had been suppressing for years and was
reluctant to open those doors for a good reason. The hurt I was
feeling from losing my wife and job was something I had only
experienced when my brother died. But grieving my brother's
death was a lot easier because I was in no way at fault. But with
my wife and job, I had to take on some of the responsibility for
the losses—a burden which made the grieving process so much
harder and longer. The last thing I wanted was to add working on
my personal issues from my youth, for this would definitely bring
more suffering to my already devastated existence. In hindsight,
the cure frightened me more than the disease; this may seem
ridiculous, I know, but it happens all the time in our lives when
our fears cripple us and prevent us from moving on to better
things.

It took a few more years before God brought me to the point
of a showdown over those locked doors in my heart. My
wounded heart needed to be mended, and the time for healing had
come.

Feeling restless one Saturday afternoon, I drove down to
the river to go for a walk to clear my head. The wind was howling

out of the north, and it was a cold, dreary day—one that fit my mood. Like I said, I had lost my wife and my job both in the same year and going for walks by myself helped me cope. This walk, in particular, started out like many others that I had taken to try to make sense of all that had happened over the last couple of years, but this walk was very different.

I soon found myself on a deserted part of the beach. I was totally alone, and the loud roar of the waves crashing onto shore was drowning out everything else around me. God set this place for me to deal with the excruciating pain of rejection that I felt at that moment and had been feeling over the years.

The pain in my life had become too much to bear. As I looked out over the lake, I contemplated if I should start swimming out until I had no more strength…then just give in and let nature take its course. I remembered how serene it was when I swam out to the nets as a teenager and almost drowned. It certainly would end my painful existence. Then I thought, *Yes, it would end my pain, but how could I do that to my kids and family?* I just couldn't be that selfish. I quickly cleared those thoughts from my head. For if those thoughts had turned into actions, the instant I breathed in the cold waters of Lake Huron, I would have been immediately standing before Jesus.

Even though He would have accepted me into His kingdom, I think He would have shown me what my life would have been like in the years to come, and what I would have missed: the great times with my kids over the last twenty years; a new love in my life and marrying that wonderful woman; the coming to the Lord of my second son and his commitment to learning and teaching

God's Word; the marriage of my oldest son, and the arrival of my grandkids. I would have missed out on all of this if I had selfishly taken my own life—not to mention the devastation it would have caused my kids, family, and friends. My children had been through too much pain already with the loss of one parent. With those thoughts behind me, never to be thought of again, I looked up into the sky to have a few honest words with God.

I had become one of His children when I received Christ. I had rights as a child of God to come to Him at any time with any problem I had. On that beach, with the wind howling and the waves crashing, it was time. I became absolutely honest with Him on how I was not impressed with where this relationship had taken me. How could someone who claimed that He loved me, as He said He did, let all this happen to me? Not only that, but seeing the pain and suffering that my kids were going through was unbearable. At this point, I epitomized the attitude of many in today's society by not wanting to take any responsibility for my actions as they related to the state in which I found myself.

After yelling at the top of my lungs at God until it was all out of my system, (it's a good thing the noise from the wind and waves drowned out my yelling, or they would have been taking me away in a straitjacket), I dropped down onto my knees in the sand. With my view on almost everything in my life askew, and my heart broken and feeling emotionally drained, a beautiful picture emerged of a loving God wrapping His arms around me and saying, "Finally, you have come to Me wholeheartedly."

It was right there that everything started to change; I realized that I was battling everything that was going on in my life with my own strength, and I had shut God out. With my heart shattered, I handed those pieces to God and humbly asked for forgiveness and help. I had nothing left to give to anyone; I was as broken as a man could be. But at that particular moment, I was where God needed me to be to begin the journey of healing my shattered heart. My pride was gone, and with it, my thoughts that I was still in control and the only one in charge of my life. Now, that was all changed.

This awareness let me begin the process of surrendering all of my will to God and making God's will for my life my primary concern for finding the peace that He had promised in **1 Corinthians 14:33** that had always eluded me: *"For God is not a God of disorder but of peace."*

The Turning Point in My Life

When I stopped trying to be the perfect Christian, I humbly yielded to the workings of the Holy Spirit. Once and for all, I started to break free of that old Ten Commandments yardstick my prideful nature was using to make me feel better about myself. Remember, my understanding of the Ten Commandments was a yardstick measurement against others who measured up shorter than me.

A *Daily Bread* reading exemplifies so perfectly the changes I should have let happen years earlier:

> "My father and I used to fell trees and cut them
> to size with a two-man crosscut saw. Being young and
> energetic, I tried to force the saw into the cut. 'Easy

does it,' my father would say, 'Let the saw do the work.'"xxx

I think of Paul's words in **Philippians 2:13:** *"It is God who works in you."* Easy does it. Let Him do the work of changing us, and that was my new objective—to be obedient to God on how He wanted me to work at bringing healing to my heart:

> **"C. S. Lewis** said that growth is much more than reading what Christ said and carrying it out. He explained, 'A real Person, Christ…is doing things to you…gradually turning you permanently into…a new little Christ, a being which…shares in His power, joy, knowledge, and eternity.'"xxxi

Perfectly put.

God's Resolve

Amazingly enough, God had already put a few things into place that were such blessings. Before my wife left, she and I were going to counselling in Port Huron with a professional counsellor named Dan. After she left, I thought to myself, I never want to be in this situation again. It was way too much pain for all who were involved. So, I decided to keep going to counselling for myself, so if I ever remarried, I would have a better chance at making it work. One thing that I have learned that is important in all relationships, whether it be with people or with God, is that you need to work at them. If you don't put in the time and the work, relationships grow cold and unsatisfying. Put in the time and work; relationships are the best thing this side of Heaven.

One of the key factors in being okay with others is being okay with yourself.

I didn't know it at the time, but that decision to keep going to counselling was one of the best decisions I ever made. With Dan's help, I dug down deep into the dark places of my heart and brought up all of my past demons that kept me in chains for so many years. Exposing these demons to the light of Christ was the only way to get rid of them. Demons do not like the light of Christ.

> *"Submit yourselves, then, to God. Resist the devil,*
> *and he will flee from you." – **James 4:7***

It was, by far, the most humbling thing that I have ever done. At one point in sharing my past, I was physically shaking as I talked about something I didn't want to deal with but had to. It took some time, but in the end, all of the weight I had been carrying around year after year lifted. Now, I'm experiencing the full forgiveness of Christ in all aspects of my life.

It was painful work, but absolutely worth it. For years, I was dying emotionally; and the ways I was trying to deal with those hurts was killing me and every relationship around me. I had so many destructive habits. Some just defeated me emotionally and physically, while others were just so time consuming, they kept me from truly putting the time and effort into my relationship with God that was needed.

24

LETTING GO OF THE PAST

Accepting forgiveness for past mistakes can be hard; for our past mistakes are usually never forgotten, only dealt with. The Lord's Prayer says, *"Forgive us our sins."* One thing I know is that the harshest and most critical person in my life is **me,** and from what I have observed, that is true in other people's lives as well. That's why it's so hard to let Christ's forgiveness work in our hearts because most times we don't feel worthy of that forgiveness. And when we don't feel worthy of that forgiveness, it makes it really hard to forgive others.

However, **Matthew 6:14** still says, *"For if you forgive others when they sin against you, your heavenly Father will also forgive you."* Letting Christ's forgiveness work in our hearts for past mistakes and forgiving others who have done wrong is key for a healthy mental and spiritual life.

Forgiveness is essential for the healing process. It's a two-part system, and both parts have to work, or it's all in vain.

Besides that, forgiveness is not a one-time deal; I have to constantly remember to ask for forgiveness, and to forgive others. Not forgiving and holding onto bitterness is corrosive. It's like taking a slow-working poison and hoping that the person you hold bitterness towards will die a terrible death. That seems extreme, but I found it to be true in a lot of ways. Bitterness over time can affect your health and your state of mind. I didn't deal with the bitterness in my heart for many years, and I paid a heavy price for it.

Refusing to allow God's forgiveness to work in our lives and refusing to extend forgiveness to others does not leave us in good standing with God. **Matthew 6:15** is clear: *"If you do not forgive others their sins, your Father will not forgive your sins."*

You can't live in this world without being hurt or hurting someone else. Many times, it's not on purpose, but as the Bible says in **James 3:8**, *"The tongue is a restless evil."* And since that restless evil comes out in my speech, there have been many times I have said things that I wish I could have pulled right back out of the air. As I have matured, and not liking to put my foot in my mouth, I try very hard to think before I speak. I may not be able to tame my tongue altogether, but I have managed to subdue it most of the time.

Because hurting each other is easy to do, forgiveness and understanding—no matter how hard they both seem—have to be a big part of who we are. One great thing I look forward to when I get to Heaven is being made perfect; all of my inadequacies will be laid down as I walk through Heaven's gates. Never again will I be worrying about offending or hurting anyone. Everyone else will be made perfect as well—thus making all relationships unbelievably easy. And I, for one, look forward to that day.

Remember once again what Vince Vitale said: "I can look back at my life as a teenager right now and say I thought at that time some of the things I did were no big deal, but the reality is they were truly terrible."[xxxii]

Some of my past memories can still come back vividly and evoke old feelings of guilt and shame. So how do I fight those feelings? I just take them to Jesus in prayer, asking Him to help me see myself as He sees me—as the forgiven man that I am. For I know His forgiveness is not just for the moment but everlasting. After that, my guilt and shame are once again laid to rest.

That's why it's so important to keep short accounts throughout your life. Try to think before you act in all situations, though I still haven't mastered that one yet. It's clear, the older one gets, that the hurts that have been caused to others throughout life are not forgotten.

When my mother was in her late eighties, I asked her one time if she had any regrets. To my surprise, she answered with, "I have nothing but regrets." I would have never thought that would have been her answer; however, as I get older, my mind returns to old memories without my consent. Out of nowhere, I think about past events concerning how hurtful or disrespectful I was or what I should have said or done—but didn't—to show my family how much I cared.

As I thought it through, my mother's answer about regrets became clear to me. The fact is, as you age, you cannot help recalling those types of memories. Even though you can't change one thing from your past, it can still paralyze you. So, what I have learned over the years is to keep short accounts—by that, I mean, instead of being inconsiderate with words or actions, do what's right. Live out **Galatians 5:22** every day: *"But the fruit of the Spirit is love, joy, peace, forbearance, kindness, goodness, faithfulness, gentleness and self-control,"* and you will never have to worry about regrets when you're older.

My humanity, that is, my actions outside of Christ, isn't going away; but if I ask the hard questions of myself at the end of each day, I will become more like Christ. I need to ask myself, for example, if my words are more critical than they need to be and, if so, what am I doing to change? Were my actions Christ-like or were they selfish in nature? Again, what am I doing to change? As I examine how I act and speak each day and humbly bring my failures to Christ, I can only become and act more like Him.

Psalm 139:23–24 says:

> *"Search me, God, and know my heart; test me and know my anxious thoughts. See if there is any offensive way in me, and lead me in the way everlasting."*

For me, it's a very hard process, but working through this process is rewarding, and the outcome is knowing that I'm changing into the image of Christ a little more each day. I'm also sharply reducing future regrets in my life, and hopefully, by continuing to do the work, at some point I won't be known as that grumpy, critical, old guy anymore.

Support Is Important

Over the years, I've done the work and held the course by relying on God's grace and His continuing guidance that keeps me on track. God's work in my life also involved some awesome people. I will always be indebted to my counsellor, Dan, for his patience and deep commitment to seeing me and others work through their inner trials.

I am also grateful to the other five guys that sat around the table in Dan's office every week. We learnt how to become better men by discussing and sharing thoughts about one another's lives; no crap was tolerated at that table, and if you weren't being totally honest, you were immediately called out on it. I found it a lot easier to call out others on honesty than to take myself to task—but I did learn to be honest with my inner self. It was hard, but learning this skill has brought me much healing and a closer walk with Christ. One of the most important lessons I learned was this: shutting down and doing the silent treatment in my relationships, with others or with God, never solves anything. In fact—it only makes the situation worse.

Once I realized that getting issues out into the open was the best policy, it became a way of life. When I started dating my present wife late in 2012, I made one thing very clear, and it was written in stone: **Men are stupid. I am not going to get it, so just tell me.** Being a man, I can do and say some boneheaded things at times and not even know it. This simple instruction to my wife (which she had no problem agreeing to) has saved me a lot of anxiety, for I always know right away when I have screwed up. Her just telling me what I did wrong makes it very easy to apologize and make it right. In addition, I'm able to learn from my mistakes and avoid repeating them. I wish all of my relationships were that easy; if I continue to ask God to search and test my heart on a daily basis, they may start to be.

With all that I have learned, I also have been able to help others who struggle with the same issues. It's amazing how God's working in our lives can have far-reaching effects into other people's lives, way beyond what we can imagine.

I also discovered that in any healing, there are times of doubt and uncertainty for the future; but by staying the course **Galatians 6:9** comes alive: *"And let us not grow weary of doing good, for in the due season we will reap, if we do not give up."* The reaping in my case was healthy relationships, being okay with myself, and the drive to continue pursuing the goal of becoming more like Christ in all avenues of my life.

God Loves Broken People

I have shared my very personal life experiences to show that God loves broken people and does not give up on them even if, to the outside world, they look okay. We don't have to be good enough to come to Jesus; it's just good that we come. That's all He wants—a relationship with us—so that He can begin healing our brokenness. He offers His forgiveness to heal our wounds, His peace to remove our anxious thoughts, and His love to give us a hope and future in Him. If you think you're not broken in some way, you would be one of the very few in this world who isn't.

The song "Just As I Am" puts it so beautifully:

Just as I am, without one plea,
But that Thy blood was shed for me,
And that Thou bid'st me come to Thee,
O Lamb of God, I come! I come!^{xxxiii}

All God asks of us is to come. He can't make it any easier than that. We're the ones who make it complicated.

You're not alone: most everyone has some type of emotional history.

Over the years and after many conversations with a lot of different people, I realized that everyone has locked up closets that are full of hurts, insecurities, and vulnerabilities they don't want to deal with or, like me, didn't know how to deal with. As I hear story after story from people growing up in dysfunctional families, I wonder if anyone ever had a well-adjusted childhood. If you were one of the lucky ones who did, cherish those memories because it doesn't seem to be the norm.

The stories I have heard from people range from not feeling loved to having to deal with devastating events beyond their control; however, looking at these people, you would never know from their outward appearance that such heartaches exist and are locked deep down in their hearts. I am aware that most people don't want to bring these hurts to the surface for all to see. I know I didn't want to be exposed as someone who was not able to deal with my past hurts or my agonizing insecurities and vulnerabilities in a positive manner. But this only made me feel lonelier and more isolated, and that caused very destructive patterns in my life. The result of trying to anesthetize the pain over the years only made it more severe and harder to deal with.

It's a fact that we all have hurts in our past. Acknowledging them is hard, and working on them is even harder; but there is no other way to find healing. I wonder if that is why some who have been presented with the Gospel of Christ and have been drawn to Him can reject His offer. Maybe in their subconscious they know that God is going to search their hearts, and the fear of being exposed and vulnerable is just too unbearable to consider. Thus, it keeps them from searching out God, which is ultimately sad because the following verses show how well God knows us.

> *"Are not two sparrows sold for a penny? Yet not one of them will fall to the ground outside your Father's care. And even the very hairs of your head are all numbered. So don't be afraid; you are worth more than many sparrows."* – **Matthew 10:29–31**

> *"You have searched me, Lord, and you know me. You know when I sit and when I rise; you perceive my thoughts from afar. You discern my going out and my lying down; you are familiar with all my ways."* – ***Psalm 139:1–3***

So, if God already knows us through and through, why shy away? No one is too far gone for God's love and the hope He offers.

> *"'For I know the plans I have for you,' declares the Lord, 'plans to prosper you and not to harm*

you, plans to give you hope and a future. Then you will call on me and come and pray to me, and I will listen to you. You will seek me and find me when you seek me with all your heart. I will be found by you,' declares the Lord, 'and will bring you back from captivity.'" – Jeremiah 29:11–14

The key to finding God has everything to do with our hearts. It's very clear from the verses above that God is more familiar with us than we are or could ever hope to be with ourselves. He wants our hearts. And as I said from the very start, my journey with God started with a sincere prayer from my heart.

Jeremiah 29:13 says, *"You will seek me and find me when you seek me with all your heart."* God is waiting on us to seek Him with all our heart, a heart which He knows intimately already. It's still our decision, though, to give it to Him; He is not going to overstep our free will. With all that God knows about us, He still longs for us to come to Him in whatever state we're in. Absolutely nothing anyone has done will tarnish God's view of us; none of us are too far gone. All of the vulnerabilities that hold us back are all exposed to God already. All we need to do, as the song states, is to come:

Just as I am, without one plea,
But that Thy blood was shed for me,
And that Thou bid'st me come to Thee,
O Lamb of God, I come! I come![xxxiv]

The song doesn't say we have to get our lives together, then come; it says, "Just as I am." More than anything, He wants to see us come to Him through Jesus Christ, so that we can be washed clean and put in proper standing in His sight.

After we come just as we are, we have a promise from God that He will break us free from the captivity of sin, and will listen to us and give us a hope and a future in Him, as **Jeremiah 29:11** promises.

God does not say that He will ridicule us for our past. He does not say that He will punish us for our past or use our insecurities and vulnerabilities to embarrass us. No, He says that we have a hope and a future in Him and only Him. Jesus has already taken the punishment for our sinful past, but He can't take that punishment from us unless we ask Him to.

I can't stress enough that God is not looking for perfect people.

> *"When Jesus heard this, He told them, 'Healthy people don't need a doctor—sick people do. I have come to call not those who think they are good, but those who know they are bad.'"* – **Mark 2:17**

God calls all those who know they are second-rate, unsatisfactory, inadequate, imperfect, worthless, wicked, immoral, corrupt, criminal, dishonest, rotten to the core, or, as the Apostle Paul called himself in **1 Timothy 1:15** *"the chief of all sinners."* Are you starting to get the gist of who God wants?

The Bible says God is not looking for those who think they are good for one simple reason: their pride prevents them from seeing their sinfulness. And if we can't see our sinfulness, we can't see the need for a Saviour. God is happy with those who won't even lift their eyes to Heaven because they think the sins they have committed are too unforgivable. God cries out to these people with perfect love, asking them to come and receive His grace.

Apostle Paul says in **Romans 5:20,** *"But the more we see our sinfulness, the more we see God's abounding grace forgiving us."* This means the more we see our sin as God sees it (destructive), the more we see His grace as abundant—forgiveness we don't deserve. The amount of God's grace is poured out in relation to our sinfulness. Some who live good and wholesome lives come to Christ because they know something is missing, which can only be filled with a relationship with Jesus Christ. These people may have an easier time transitioning to be more like Christ than others who come to Christ from a hard life of sin.

That's why God's grace is being poured out in great amounts daily in my life, while in others this may not be the case. Only God sees the sinfulness of the heart. The equation is very simple: the greater the sins, the greater God's abounding grace is poured out to His glory.

It doesn't matter if you are Mary, the mother of Jesus, who still had to accept Jesus as her Saviour; she had to make that choice like anyone else, for her free will to choose was no different than yours or mine. It's no different if you are the criminal being crucified beside Jesus, to whom Jesus said after he asked for forgiveness, *"Today you will be with me in paradise"* **(Luke 23:43).** It's no different no matter who you are. God's grace will cover all sinners' sins if they simply ask Him for forgiveness.

25

LIFE CRISIS

Self-righteousness and self-pity are a cancer to the soul.

The Parable of the Pharisee

A Pharisee was a self-righteous or hypocritical person who claimed to have superior spirituality to most everyone, and especially to a Jewish tax collector. The Jewish tax collector was despised and hated by fellow Jews for collecting taxes for the Roman government; in addition to that, he was considered a thief for overcharging and pocketing the difference.

The Parable

"To some who were confident of their own righteousness and looked down on everyone else, Jesus told this parable: 'Two men went up to the temple to pray, one a Pharisee and the other a tax

collector. The Pharisee stood by himself and prayed: "God, I thank you that I am not like other people—robbers, evildoers, adulterers—or even like this tax collector. I fast twice a week and give a tenth of all I get." But the tax collector stood at a distance. He would not even look up to heaven, but beat his breast and said, "God, have mercy on me, a sinner." I tell you that this man (the tax collector), rather than the other, went home justified before God. For all those who exalt themselves will be humbled, and those who humble themselves will be exalted.'" – **Luke 18:9–14**

This parable shows no one is above or below God's forgiveness. If you identify with the Pharisee, you humble yourself to God's grace. If you identify with the tax collector, great—Jesus says those who humble themselves will find God's grace. But be cautious not to turn your unworthiness into an excuse for thinking yourself too unworthy to come to God to accept His grace. That's self-pity, which is just another form of pridefulness.

I once met a man facing what could have been life-threatening health issues. He was going to have a test done in the near future. When talking with him, I asked him about praying for his situation, and he told me that he didn't feel right about coming to God because of his health crisis. He felt that he was too unworthy to even ask for God's help. His understanding of God was formed by a religion of guilt, which told him that his worthiness was derived from keeping the Ten Commandments, a task that he, I, or anyone else could never achieve.

His inability to keep the Ten Commandments showed him that he was unworthy in God's sight. But instead of using this knowledge of unworthiness to come and accept God's grace through Jesus Christ—the opposite happened; he stayed away. God was calling him through this crisis in his life to show him not to rely on himself, but to become a child of God and to lay hold of the promises given in **Hebrews 4:16:** *"Let us then approach God's throne of grace with confidence, so that we may receive mercy and find grace to help us in our time of need."*

The sad part of this story is that the very thing God was using to draw him into the kingdom of Heaven was the very thing he was using to keep himself out, showing the pridefulness of self-pity.

God uses dire situations throughout the Bible to get people's attention so that they will repent and turn to Him or come back into fellowship with Him. Nothing has changed; God still uses extremely serious or urgent situations in our lives to wake us up in our time of need to call upon Him for help. God's concern is that we call out to Him, not why we're calling out to Him. Like a loving father, all He desires is to show His love and compassion towards us, for us to be in fellowship with Him, or if we have strayed, to come back into fellowship.

When God Is Knocking at the Door

> *"Look! I have been standing at the door, and I am*
> *constantly knocking. If anyone hears me calling*

him and opens the door, I will come in and
fellowship with him and he with me." –
Revelation 3:20

Paul, a salesman who usually stopped by the shop on a weekly basis, suddenly stopped showing up, and we found out from his boss that Paul had a sudden heart problem. A month later, Paul was back on his route and shared with us what happened. Paul told us that he had had some chest pains, which didn't seem too serious, but were concerning, so to be on the safe side he went to the hospital to get checked out. At the hospital, they found that his heart had severe blockages and immediately rushed him into surgery—a measure which saved his life.

In a consultation with the surgeon a few days later, Paul learned of the seriousness of his situation. The surgeon told him that people who had this kind of heart condition typically don't survive because the pain associated with that type of heart attack masks the seriousness of the problem. Most don't get treatment in time, dying before they make it to the hospital. This news had a profound effect on Paul; subsequently, he quit smoking and started eating right, exercising, and praying.

Because of the crisis in Paul's life, he was hearing Jesus knocking at the door of his heart as in **Revelation 3:20:** *"Look! I have been standing at the door, and I am constantly knocking."* Paul opened that door a sliver, not enough to let Jesus in, but just enough to comfort himself with the knowledge that Jesus was there.

On one of Paul's weekly visits, we talked about what happened in his life after his surgery. Paul shared with me how grateful he was to God for sparing his life and all the changes that he was making. I told him that I would pray for him, which I did, and gave him a copy of the **Book of John** from the Bible, which he told me that he was excited to read. The following week when he came back, he was still going strong on eating right and exercising, but the talk about God was a little less.

Another book I had given him, *One Minute After You Die* by Erwin W. Lutzer, explains in detail what happens to someone after he or she dies with or without Christ. He promised to read it. But when he dropped by the next week, and I asked him how he was progressing with the book. He told me that it was still in his car, but he was going to read it. In the following weeks, when Paul stopped by, the conversation reverted to the same banter we had been exchanging before his heart attack. It seemed to me that Paul had forgotten the dread of his ordeal. The door which Christ was knocking on was still open a little, but any urgency Paul had felt to find out more about God appeared not to be as intense.

Fortunately, the Holy Spirit was working in Paul's heart, and the intensity I thought was diminishing was really growing stronger. He was still reading the **Book of John,** seeking answers, and asking very specific questions about God, faith, and the afterlife. I don't know if Christ went from "I am constantly knocking" to banging on the door of his recently surgically repaired heart, but the door of Paul's heart was flung wide open on a Tuesday afternoon in January 2021 when Paul accepted Jesus' offer of forgiveness, eliminating his debt of sin.

> *"If anyone hears me calling him and opens the door, I will come in and fellowship with him and he with me."* – **Revelation 3:20**

The moment Paul prayed to ask for forgiveness, in God's eyes, all of Paul's impurities were washed away by the blood of the Lamb, Jesus Christ. Paul's name is now written in the Lamb's Book of Life. Now, Paul is a new man in Christ with his final destination set in stone—Heaven.

The Apostle John's vision given to him by God:

> *"Nothing impure will ever enter it (Heaven), nor will anyone who does what is shameful or deceitful, but only those whose names are written in the Lamb's book of life."* – **Revelation 21:27**

Paul has received an awesome promise and begun a relationship with Jesus here on earth, a friendship like no other, and has been given the privilege of learning to become more like Jesus.

26

DECISION FOR CHRIST?

Now Is the Time

2 Corinthians 6:2 says, *"For he says, 'In the time of my favour I heard you, and in the day of salvation I helped you.' I tell you, now is the time of God's favour, now is the day of salvation."* **Salvation is our choice, but the offer of salvation does have a shelf life.**

At times, I just wonder what it will take for some to swallow their pride and accept Christ. For me, it took a few times of looking death in the face before I humbled myself before God and asked for forgiveness through what Jesus did on the cross. **What will it take in your life?**

Jesus invites us into a relationship with Himself, but relationships exist only if both parties say yes. If you are not willing to say yes, Jesus can do nothing on His side. Don't be foolish in thinking there will always be time to find God. As I get older, a truth that becomes more and more apparent to me is that time flies. For that reason, the Lord warns us in **2 Corinthian 6:2,** *"Now is the day of salvation."*

God's Grace Has a Time Limit

> *"He isn't really being slow about his promised*
> *return, even though it sometimes seems that way.*
> *But he is waiting, for the good reason that he is*
> *not willing that any should perish, and he is giving*
> *more time for sinners to repent." –* **2 Peter 3:9**

Be careful not to think there will always be enough time to decide if what is written here in these pages has any merit or not because there are two things that are absolutely true: a non-decision is a **no** decision, and a decision put off too long could become a **no** decision because of circumstances.

Opportunity Missed

A good example of waiting too long and having it turn into a no decision is tragically characterized by some of the passengers on the RMS Titanic on the night of April 12, 1912. Waiting too long to decide if they should get into the lifeboats after the Titanic hit an iceberg became a **no** decision for many. The book, *The Titanic's Last Hero*, is a testimony to John Harper, a pastor from Scotland who died the night the Titanic sank. He was helping people see the need of Christ before the Titanic sank and they died. It's recorded that more than 1,500 men, women, and children tragically lost their lives when the ship sank after hitting an iceberg. Shockingly, many who perished had refused to board the lifeboats at first, believing the ship was truly indestructible and unsinkable.

How many people today are not reading the signs that Christ is coming back? How many truly believe there will be no judgement and no accountability— that life is just going to continue as it is? I am not a doomsday person, but Bible prophecies are lining up, and the world should take notice. Everyone should take heed and find the lifeboat of salvation before time runs out.

Can you imagine the look of dread on the faces of those who refused to get into the lifeboats, as they stood on the deck of the Titanic holding onto the guardrail for dear life? Do you wonder what thoughts raced through their minds as the ship was slipping into the sea? I imagine there was probably regret that their chance of being rescued from certain death was being rowed away by the men in the lifeboats they refused to board.

Only two options exist for leaving this world: you can leave with Jesus when he comes back at the Rapture, or you can leave in death. Either way, you have a standing appointment before God one day, and no one other than God knows when that day will be. That should be a very sobering thought.

Remember the first page of my testimony: My mom was at the door in the front room speaking in a hushed voice with a very distinguished man. She then came into the living room, motioned for me to sit on the couch with her, and sat down facing me. Tenderly, in a very soft tone, she told me that Steve, my older brother by six years with whom I shared a bedroom, had been killed in a car accident around midnight. Steve had been with his friends, riding in the passenger seat, when a drunk driver went through an intersection and slammed into their car. Seat belts weren't worn in those days, and Steve had flown out of the car, hit his head on a traffic light pole, and died instantly.

I will never forget the memory of that night; furthermore, I will also never forget the fact that neither Steve, nor I, nor anyone else that night knew beforehand that when Steve left the house, he would never return. It shows us that we never know when our time is up. That's why Jesus, in "The Parable of the Rich Fool" in **Luke 12:20,** says this: *"But God said to him, 'You fool! This very night your life will be demanded from you.'"* And once your life is demanded by God, it's done. You had better have your affairs concerning who God is in order, for as it is stated in **Hebrews 9:27,** life is a one-time deal: *"And as it is appointed unto men once to die, but after this the judgment."*

Even though God is a loving God, He is also a just God; so don't gamble on where you're going to spend eternity. His patience will run out one day, so take heed, for there will be a time when the offer of grace is off the table. **There are no second chances once you've taken your last breath.**

I make no apologies for being adamant about the truths written here which, as you can see, I believe with all my heart and soul. I just want all those who read this book to search out the truth for themselves, and the best way to find truth is to ask God to open your heart by the Holy Spirit. I am not trying to badger anyone into a decision, for God gave us free will to decide what belief system we will choose to live our lives by; but to be perfectly blunt, a belief system that doesn't deal with the sinfulness of man is a belief system that will lead you right to Hell.

One thing that I have learned in life is that our beliefs have a direct and profound effect on how we act and feel. For over twenty years of my life, I felt sure that there was a moral God, but I wasn't living as if I did—and this caused me to be out of sync with what I believed. Living inconsistently with my belief system was causing a lack of peace and harmony in my life.

As I said before, everything I had experienced up to this point in my life had left me unfulfilled and pondering the age-old questions of life itself. If I'd had peace and harmony in my life at that time, I don't think I would have found God through Jesus Christ; for if I'd had peace and harmony, why would I have been looking for God in the first place?

Making any decision about God shouldn't come from being pressured, and I know it seems that I am putting on the pressure here; however, to me, it's more about the seriousness of the subject than it is about pressuring anyone for a decision. I just want to make sure that whoever reads this knows they have, as the Bible states so clearly, only two options for the hereafter: **Heaven or Hell**. And since we are born into sin, and the punishment for sin has already been set before we were born, the only option given to us is actually the of choice of **Heaven.**

The Persuading Power of Hell

The fact that I believed there was a Hell persuaded me to believe in Jesus Christ. I want to return to the subject of Hell because it's the hardest concept in the Bible for mankind to accept. If anyone says differently, I would say that person's heart is a little hardened towards the lost—those who choose to end up there. The importance of a Hell, in a way, magnifies the significant difference of right and wrong and the separation that God puts between the two. Just as the words associated with *right* (just, fair, ethical, honest, moral, righteous, honourable) starkly contrast with those words associated with *wrong* (bad, unethical, illegal, immoral, wicked, dishonest, unrighteous), in the human race, these words and our behaviour concerning them are often interchanged because of our sinfulness. This gives us the illusion that the mixture of right and wrong is okay, as long as the rights outweigh the wrongs. In God's Heaven, this is not the case; there is no mixing of right and wrong. Nothing associated with wrong will be in Heaven, and nothing associated with right will be in Hell.

Hell was the very factor that led me away from wrong and brought me to being right in God's eyes through the work of what Christ did on the cross. Hell was the catalyst in my life that made me search out God. I'm glad that having a hard time with the concept of Hell didn't sway me to disregard the reality of it, for to disregard the reality of Hell, I would have to disregard the reality of Heaven and even the reality of who God says He is.

As Heaven is woven into the Word of God, Hell is also. To erase Hell from the Word of God, I would have to change my perception of who God says He is, and that would discredit God's holiness and perfect judgements. To discredit God is to take away His Godship, which makes Him out to be *a* god, and not *the* God. So, if God is just *a* god, then why would I ever spend my life giving my whole allegiance to Him?

The God with whom I have a relationship is *the God of the Bible,* and since He is unable to misrepresent truth, then I have to accept the existence of Hell on His Word alone and be thankful that I can be pardoned from it.

Remember, our rationale when it comes to the subject of Heaven and Hell is limited, but God's is not:

> *"For my thoughts are not your thoughts, neither are your ways my ways, declares the Lord. For as the heavens are higher than the earth, so are my ways higher than your ways and my thoughts than your thoughts." – **Isaiah 55:8–9***

So, on our part, that's where faith comes into play—the faith to believe that God is the one and only true God and that all that is written in the Bible is true, including writings on the subject of Hell. If you still think that there is wiggle room on any subject written in God's Word, let's look at how God responded to Job when Job was questioning God about His motives in **Job 38.**

Prologue: Job

The back story here is that Job was very faithful to God in all aspects of his life. In **Job 1:8**, this is what God said about him: *"Have you considered my servant Job? There is no one on earth like him; he is blameless and upright, a man who fears God and shuns evil."*

One day, God was telling Satan about His servant, Job, to which Satan replied in **Job 1:10–11**, *"It's easy for him to follow you when you have put a hedge of protection around him and* *everything he has, but if that hedge wasn't there, Job would curse you to your face."* God let Satan test Job, but not to the point of death. After Job's trials and tribulations, which God allowed Satan to execute, Job wanted to put God on the hot seat about the fairness of his ordeal.

Retribution Theology

"For in our thinking, we tend to believe in the doctrine of 'retribution theology.' This means that every act receives just punishment or a just reward in this present life; for example, we should be able to tell who is righteous or who is wicked by whether they are visibly blessed or cursed here on earth. This is a false doctrine, but Job thought it should be true and went on the offensive, charging God with injustice and calling for a trial. God condescends and agrees to be put on trial (gotquestions.org)."[xxxv]

God on Trial

The verses below (from the Book of Job) give an overview of how God responded to Job after Job questioned Him about the fairness of his suffering from the hand of Satan. God's response continues for a few chapters, but these verses clearly show us that God is totally in control.

"Then the Lord spoke to Job out of the storm. He said: 'Who is this that obscures my plans with words without knowledge? Brace yourself like a man; I will question you, and you shall answer me.

Where were you when I laid the earth's foundation? Tell me, if you understand. Who marked off its dimensions? Surely you know! Who stretched a measuring line across it? On what were its footings set, or who laid its cornerstone— while the morning stars sang together and all the angels shouted for joy?'" – **Job 38:1–7**

"'What is the way to the abode of light? And where does darkness reside? Can you take them to their places? Do you know the paths to their dwellings? Surely you know, for you were already born! You have lived so many years!'" – **Job 38:19–21**

"The Lord said to Job 'Will the one who contends with the Almighty correct him? Let him who accuses God answer him!' Then Job answered the Lord: 'I am unworthy—how can I reply to you? I put my hand over my mouth. I spoke once, but I have no answer—twice, but I will say no more.' Then the Lord spoke to Job out of the storm: 'Brace yourself like a man; I will question you, and you shall answer me. Would you discredit my justice? Would you condemn me to justify yourself? Do you have an arm like God's, and can your voice thunder like his? Then adorn yourself with glory and splendour, and clothe yourself in honour and majesty. Unleash the fury of your wrath, look at all who are proud and bring them

low, look at all who are proud and humble them, crush the wicked where they stand. Bury them all in the dust together; shroud their faces in the grave. Then I myself will admit to you that your own right hand can save you.'" – **Job 40:1–14**

Job wanted answers about why God let these tragic events happen to him, so God let Job question Him like He was on trial. God answered Job by asking him a few questions which were way beyond Job's scope of understanding. When God started to speak, Job, being a smart man, realized very quickly that he should never have tried to challenge God. Job put his hand over his mouth and just listened. God made it very clear—He is quite able to run His universe with power and majesty and integrity that is beyond reproach.

Are we going to be like Job, putting God on trial for things that we don't understand—things like Hell? Or are we going to put God on trial for problems in our lives that we can't comprehend why God let happen?

If so, do you think God's response would be any different from how He responded to Job? For those who assume that they are on the same level as God, thinking that you will be able to look God directly in the eye and reprimand Him, take notice of how Job responded:

"Then Job answered the Lord: 'I am unworthy— how can I reply to you? I put my hand over my mouth. I spoke once, but I have no answer—twice, but I will say no more.'" – ***Job 40:3–5***

Those who think that all that has been written on these pages is just foolishness and mere fantasy will one day be awakened to the undeniable fact: no one is going to contest God's power and majesty. What He says is going to stand.

On the topic of His Word, not one letter will be deleted on any subject: *"Heaven and earth will disintegrate before even the smallest detail of the word of God will fail or lose its power"* **(Luke 16:17).**

Is God Uncaring?

Some could very well have that view, but it comes from a lack of understanding of who God is and the sinful world in which we live. This is highlighted in the Book of Job.

In light of Job's trials, God might seem a little dismissive or lacking in compassion based on His response to all that Job suffered as He asked, *"Who is this that obscures My plans with words without knowledge?"* **(Job 38:2)** and *"Would you discredit My justice?"* **(Job 40:8)** and *"Would you condemn Me to justify yourself?"* **(Job 40:8).**

But the way Job was responding to God about his trials was, in fact, criticizing God's character. God put a spotlight on Job's lack of understanding by the questions He asked. Job perceived his mistake very quickly and apologized: *"I know that you can do all things; no purpose of yours can be thwarted. You asked, 'Who is this that obscures My plans without knowledge?' Surely I spoke of things I did not understand, things too wonderful for me to know"* **(Job 42:1–3b).**

Through those trials, Job learned some very valuable lessons. I know that, in the most difficult times of my life, I was able to develop trust in God that I would never have found otherwise. So trials, which are never pleasant, usually bring about the greatest growth in our Christian lives, with long-lasting blessing attached. So, is God uncaring? **No.** For **Hebrews 4:15–16** says:

> *"For we do not have a high priest (Jesus) who is unable to empathize with our weaknesses, but we have one who has been tempted in every way, just as we are—yet He did not sin. Let us then approach God's throne of grace with confidence, so that we may receive mercy and find grace to help us in our time of need."*

One thing God sarcastically pointed out to Job was, *"Then I myself will admit to you that your own right hand can save you"* **(Job 40:14).** We can't save ourselves. We need God. And in my life, I have learned that when I leaned on God through the times in my life when nothing made sense, the outcome was always a renewed and stronger faith. Don't let your lack of understanding regarding God's ways put bitterness in your heart when life gets rough, for it's in those tough times when God's mercy and love shine their brightest.

Accepting Fundamental Truths

One night, on the third-story balcony of my friend's apartment, two of my closest friends and I were sitting together, enjoying each other's company and shooting the breeze about life in general. It was a warm summer night with clear skies. Looking up into the night sky, we started to admire the bright, shining stars over our heads. This prompted a conversation about the vastness of space. We were in our early twenties, and everyone at that age is some type of a philosopher; trying to be perceived as one by my friends, I brought up the fact that space goes on forever and has no ending. I stared pensively into the night sky, posing as if I knew more about the subject than I really did. This started quite the conversation.

One of my friends could not comprehend the infinity of space. No matter how hard we tried to explain it to him, he couldn't wrap his mind around it; and at that point, no one was gazing into the heavens and talking softly. We had become headstrong, young guys, ganging up on the one friend who couldn't grasp the concept of the infinity of space. Sarcastically, I asked him what was at the end of space, "a brick wall?"

"Yea, a brick wall," he replied.

"Really?" I proceeded to my next question: "What is on the other side of the brick wall?" After I asked that question, he'd had enough. He wasn't going to be persuaded that space had no ending and that was that. I know it's hard to comprehend—the infinity of space—but logic dictates that there is no other feasible explanation.

My point for telling this story is that no matter how much evidence there is to support a truth, there will always be those who cannot or will not connect the dots. Unfortunately, these people also don't even take the time to search out the evidence or the answers in any shape or form— much like my friend who couldn't wrap his mind around the infinity of space and was seemingly okay with just pushing it out of his consciousness. He hasn't changed much; and years later, when I brought up the subject of God, Heaven and Hell, and the eternity of both, he was not going to be persuaded about anything he couldn't see or touch. Whether he believes space goes on forever or not dwindles in comparison to his disregard of the reality of Heaven and Hell and where his eternal soul will end up.

For those of you like my friend who won't be persuaded that there is a God, a Heaven, and a Hell, you have a problem. Putting all your eggs in one basket— in this case, that there is no God, and that this life is all there is—means that dying has to be the ultimate tragedy, especially if you die young or if you don't get to live your life to the fullest. I can't even imagine the depression a person would experience if having to live life with a debilitating disease, thinking this life is all there is, with no hope for a future after death. That seems quite bleak to me.

I think reasoning God out of existence would make it very easy and even logical to live life any way you see fit, mostly for your own prosperity. The premise, therefore, is that you become number one, and your thinking starts to revolve only around whatever makes you feel good about yourself. Right is what you say it is, and you justify your actions based on the approval of those whom you have swayed to your line of thinking. But in the end, to whom are you going to be accountable? Can anyone feed the appetite of self-living? How would love ever survive in such an environment of entitlement? Contentment would be sought after but never found—and you would remain just a restless spirit, always looking for greener grass.

The Other Side of the Fence

Without contentment in life, you will be influenced by the "other side of the fence" dilemma. I'm sure you have heard it said that, "the grass is always greener on the other side of the fence." But a wise man pointed out to me why the grass is always greener on the other side. It's greener because it lays over top of a septic tank, and at some point, all septic tanks start to seep. I have known a few who have jumped the fence onto the lush, green grass, only to find the stench of a leaky septic tank. Then they found that there was no jumping back; they became trapped once again by their wants and desires.

From what I can see so far, those who have taken God out of the picture and live by the premise that whatever feels good must be right are always looking for that greener grass. This is an attitude that hasn't done our society a whole lot of good.

Leaving it up to individual groups to set down the new right and wrong doesn't seem to have produced a coherent standard for all to live by. As I wrote in the introduction, I like mechanics because I can follow the patterns of information to the same conclusion every time, which gives me the necessary tools to restore anything back to good working order. God's design pattern in the Bible for how we are to live is the information that, when followed correctly, keeps chaos at bay and is good for the whole of society, not just a select few.

I wish for the sake of my friend and many others that reducing God's influence, or not believing in *the God of the Bible* at all, would work out for the betterment of society. But if I were able to convince myself of that, then I would have to bring myself to believe that space ends with a brick wall!

Honestly, I don't fully understand everything about God. If I did, I guess I wouldn't need faith. But there will come a day when all will be revealed, as the Apostle Paul tells us: *"For now we see only a reflection as in a mirror; then we shall see face to face. Now I know in part; then I shall know fully, even as I am fully known"* **(1 Corinthians 13:12).** I think the reality here is that in our human state, we couldn't handle knowing fully all the things of God. That's why those mysteries are reserved for Heaven.

Even though I have unanswered questions, I am not going to ignore what I have come to know as truth concerning God. I am not going to follow every false desire that wants me to believe there is supposedly something better or easier than following God. It requires faith to bridge the gap between what is known and what hasn't yet been revealed. That is why I know that only faith and trust are going to get me to the finish line; that's why I need to run the race of life in Christ with purpose and dedication.

27

AMBASSADORS FOR CHRIST

The Race

The Apostle Paul wrote in **1 Corinthians 9:24–27**:

"In a race everyone runs, but only one person gets first prize. So run your race to win. To win the contest you must deny yourselves many things that would keep you from doing your best. An athlete goes to all this trouble just to win a blue ribbon or a silver cup, but we do it for a heavenly reward that never disappears. So I run straight to the goal with purpose in every step. I fight to win. I'm not just shadowboxing or playing around. Like an athlete I punish my body, treating it roughly, training it to do what it should, not what it wants to. Otherwise I fear that after enlisting

*others for the race, I myself might be declared
unfit and ordered to stand aside."*

I have trained hard for many different sports throughout my life. But winning a trophy or a ribbon or just having my name on a piece of paper ranking me better than a few others was always short-lived gratification. By boasting about prior achievements to keep those moments alive, I seemed to annoy my fellow athletes and basically anyone else that I trapped into listening to me. As I said before, I have some issues with pride. One thing I do know is true: if I run the race of life humbly for God, I will hear Him say at the finish line, just as in **Matthew 25:23,** *"Well done, good and faithful servant!"* And that will ring in my ears for the rest of eternity. I just can't ask any more than that from a God who has given me so much at the great expense of His Son dying on the cross for the sins of all who have chosen to believe. I am overjoyed to be one of those who believe. Jesus Christ has done for me what I could not do for myself— paid my debt of sin in full and healed my life. I will be indebted to Him for His kindness for eternity.

Out of appreciation for Jesus' kindness towards me, I want to be a faithful ambassador for Him. As Christians, we are to be ambassadors for Christ: representatives to those who don't know Him. Our role is to bring the story of forgiveness and redemption to the world by sharing God's Word with an attitude of love. We are also to share by our daily conduct, because how we live means more than what we say in many cases.

Dwight L. Moody put it this way: "Where one man reads the Bible, a hundred read you and me."[xxxvi] I cringe when I think about how many people have read me and found a poor ambassador for Christ at times; however, please don't let my poor witness, or the poor witness of any Christians or so-called Christians, sway you from receiving the greatest gift ever given: **salvation.**

In some cases, I think anything would have done a better job of getting God's Word out than man. Still, God chooses us to do the job, even with all our imperfections.

Hypocrites Can Be Found Anywhere

My ambassadorship for Jesus Christ has not always gone so well, probably making me look like a hypocrite at times. Throughout this whole book, I have been talking about a personal relationship with God through Jesus Christ. It is a relationship that doesn't disappoint, but I can't deny the fact that some religions, as well as so-called Christians, and even those who are true believers have lost their way and reflected very poorly on who God really is. It grieves my heart to see all the wrong that has been done in the name of Christianity, and it grieves God too. Why do some who know better make a mockery of the faith, plain and simple? For all kinds of reasons, people lapse into sinfulness and let themselves get ensnared into sinful behaviour.

A few times that I am not proud of, my testimony was a hindrance to those trying get a glimpse of what God is like and what He can do in a Christian's life. One of William J. Toms' quotes hits the nail on the head regarding why a Christian should live every day for God: "Be careful how you live. You may be the only Bible a person ever reads." [xxxvii] Again, the demonstration of our faith, by daily living, is very important—probably more than we know.

Free Will Is a Blessing and a Curse

It's a blessing when you use it to love your God with all your heart, soul, and mind, and when you use it to love your neighbour as yourself. But it's a curse when you use it to either accidentally or selfishly hurt others, and it is definitely a great hindrance when you use it to turn away from God.

As long as there are people who want only to feed their own egos with power, it doesn't matter what organization they are a part of; they will use others as pawns, and Christian organizations are not immune to such people. So, if you're looking for perfect people in any Christian-based organization, I don't think you would be happy even if you found them. For unless you're perfect—which I'm quite sure you're not—being around perfect people would be really annoying.

This world loves to pick apart everything from the Lazy Boy chair in the basement while reading tidbits of information on a computer screen. But in the real world, where the work is done by imperfect people, show some grace; we all have baggage we drag around, and if you're honest, you do too. My dad said to me many times, "Mike, it doesn't matter that you do a hundred things right; the only things people will remember are the things you did wrong. So don't be one of those petty people."

As I said before, no one is going to be perfect this side of Heaven, but we are perfect in God's eyes through Jesus Christ. So by God's grace, this imperfect person lives on.

The Key Is Keeping Your Eyes on Jesus

For a time in my Christian life, I let the imperfections of other believers hinder my joy. You might wonder what I mean by that statement. Since Christ is the only perfect one and His example is what we are to follow, measuring other Christians by His perfect standard means that faults are going to be seen. Being new to the faith, I wanted to be perfect in Christ, and I wanted those I admired to be perfect as well. I thought, if they weren't, **what was Christianity all about?**

My joy was lost for a while when I took my eyes off Jesus and put them on my fellow believers. But it came back when I started to see those believers for who they really were—sinners like myself who had been saved by God's grace, working on their imperfections as the Holy Spirit worked in their lives.

The older I get, the clearer I see my imperfections (my wife and kids keep me honest in that task). I have to consistently keep my character flaws in check, and with so many of my own character flaws, I can't justify judging anyone else's—so I try not to. But to be honest, it's hard at times because it's easier to look outward than inward.

After I broke down all of the pedestals upon which I had placed my fellow believers, I found **what Christianity was all about**—it's flawed people being made into the image of Christ through the work of the Holy Spirit. It's keeping our eyes on Jesus and not on the actions of anyone else, who are very likely just as imperfect as we are. The mistake I made was putting those whom I admired in the faith on equal terms with the perfect Jesus. This was very unfair to them, for they weren't perfect; and it didn't take long before their imperfections shone brightly, causing me to stumble in my faith.

But I learned a very important lesson: people are imperfect, as am I, and I need to see past their imperfections to what God is doing and has done in their lives. For everyone has a story and a past that they're working through, and I am no different. That's why it is so important to keep your eyes on Jesus, for He never disappoints, and try to see others through His eyes.

So, I learned that when keeping my eyes on Jesus and only focusing on Him, I am able to pay more attention to the importance of **Philippians 3:13–14:** *"Forgetting what lies behind and reaching forward to what lies ahead, I press on toward the goal for the prize of the upward call of God in Christ Jesus."* It's good to have fellowship with other believers and to encourage one another, but again, only Jesus is perfect.

How Gratitude Should Affect the Way We Live

In the movie *Saving Private Ryan,* an emotional scene at the end of the movie gives a clear illustration of how gratitude and appreciation for a gift that can't be repaid can be expressed by letting the magnitude of the gift dictate the way a man lives his life.

In World War Two, a mother contacts the U.S. government to plead her case. She is adamant that her son, James Ryan, must be released from his duties to return home. Why? Mrs. Ryan's three sons had joined the army, and two of them had already been killed in action. She felt she would not have the strength to endure the grief of losing a third. The army had compassion on her unfortunate situation and granted her request. Captain Miller and eight other soldiers were given the task of going through war-torn Europe to find James Ryan and get him home.

When they found Private Ryan, his platoon was holding a bridge that they had taken from the Germans. The fighting was fierce; both sides were in a deadlock, and each side had incurred many casualties. Captain Miller, over the sounds of gun and mortar fire, explained to Private Ryan that his men and he had come to get him out of there and take him home. Private Ryan refused to leave his platoon while they were under heavy fire, so Captain Miller and the eight other soldiers with him stayed and fought. This decision cost Captain Miller and seven of his fellow soldiers under his command their lives in the summer of 1944.

More than forty years later, the scene shows James Ryan and his family standing in an Army cemetery in Europe. Row after row of white crosses stretch as far as the eye can see. James Ryan is in his late sixties as he stands over the grave of Captain Miller and quietly remembers what took place over four decades earlier. James looks down at a grave and starts talking as if he were talking directly to Captain Miller. "Every day, I think of what you said to me on that bridge—'James…earn this,'—and then earn it. I tried to live my life the best I could; I hope that was enough. I hope in your eyes I earned what all of you did to rescue me that day." Ryan then turns to his wife. "Tell me I have led a good life. Tell me I am a good man." She responds, "You are a good man."[xxxviii]

What "works" could James Ryan possibly have done to match the sacrifice made by those men? None. What he did do, though, was live his life the best he could—a life they would find pleasing and honouring to their sacrifice. It wasn't payment for what they did, but an expression of appreciation and gratitude—a tribute to such brave men.

We can never pay the debt Christ paid for us on the cross. His sacrificial work on the cross for us to be forgiven is by grace only, and you can't earn grace; you can only accept it. With that in mind, what we can do is copy what James Ryan did—live a life pleasing to Him who sacrificed all on our behalf. In our case, we can do this by imitating the life of Jesus Christ throughout our lives while here on earth.

Becoming more like Christ in God's eyes is the greatest display of gratitude and appreciation for His gift of salvation. Just as Captain Ryan and the other soldiers were following orders, Jesus Christ was obediently following God's plan of love towards us: *"But God demonstrates His own love for us in this: while we were still sinners, Christ died for us"* **(Romans 5:8).**

Jesus' sacrifice was a gift of choice from Him to us. If we accept His gift, then our appreciation and gratitude should be shown by living a life pleasing to God for all to see.

To sum it all up, **Jesus Christ** was crucified on our behalf. He was raised up from the dead on the third day and is now sitting at the right hand of God. Jesus loves you and me enough to die for us—offering us eternal life, an offer that can only be accepted personally. I hope and pray that you have read anything that has pricked your heart about a relationship with Christ, that you won't disregard the conviction of the Holy Spirit. Consider putting away your pride ("I'll decide what's right and wrong. I'll run my own life. I'll sit on the throne of my heart. I'll make my own decisions. I'll do what I want to do. I'll go where I want to go. I'll be what I want to be.") Humble yourself before God. Ask Christ to cleanse your heart and clear you of all coming judgements by His grace and live your life for Him, as a free man—a person who is Heaven-bound.

28

GOD'S PROMISES

G od says, *"What I have said, that I will bring about; what I have planned, that I will do"* **(Isaiah 46:11).** In our lives, we have all experienced broken promises—either by breaking promises we made or having promises broken that were made to us. Unfortunately, in today's society, broken promises seem to be the norm.

Could you imagine what it would be like if everyone lived out what's written in **Psalm 15:4?** *"(The person) who keeps a promise even if it hurts, and does not change their mind."* Taking the time to actually think through all that would be required to fulfill a promise before committing to it would definitely have a direct influence on any promises we would ever make.

A promise made should be a promise kept, even when the unexpected happens. I made a promise to help an old friend who was in need by offering him an older car I had just bought. The car didn't cost me much and seemed to be in good working condition. When fixing it up to pass the government safety check, though, I found out the engine had a problem; it needed a cylinder head, which was a very expensive repair.

I really wasn't planning on being that generous, so my inner voice tried to talk me out of keeping my promise. I remember thinking, "It's not my fault he came upon hard times; it's not my fault the engine needs major repairs; he will understand why I am backing out of my promise." That last statement is the one that convicted me—"He will understand why I am backing out of my promise"—because it stated the truth of the matter: I was trying to back out of a promise given. I am glad I kept my promise and fixed up the engine and gave him the car, keeping my integrity intact. Trying to hang on to money when I really was in a position to give would not have justified going back on my word.

If you were to fully adopt the position of a promise made is a promise kept, would that change the way you live, or would there be hardly any change at all?

Imagine what it would be like to be able to trust every promise given—wouldn't that be awesome? But as long as man is in his sinful state, that is never going to happen. I don't know anyone, myself included, who hasn't fallen short in keeping promises. But thanks be to *the God of the Bible,* He has never broken a promise. **Hebrews 6:18** tells us, *"It is impossible for God to lie,"* and if it is impossible for God to lie, then it would be impossible for Him to break a promise.

That is why a promise should never be frivolously made; but unfortunately, many people are guilty of doing just that. A promise should always be kept as God intends—even when it hurts, without changing your mind.

Sources say that there are 8,810 promises in the Bible from God, and 7,487 of those promises are made from God to mankind. Not all of the promises God makes to mankind are good for a sinful world—such as promises of judgement, punishment, and Hell. But the promises for salvation, fellowship, friendship, hope, peace, and purpose for life, just to name a few, can be claimed by anyone with a personal relationship with Jesus Christ.

In **Numbers 23:19,** it's made very clear why God is unable to break a promise—any promise.

> *"God is not man, that he should lie, or a son of man, that he should change his mind. Has he said, and will he not do it? Or has he spoken, and will he not fulfill it?"*

Remember **Psalm 15:4** when God talks about the person who keeps a promise even if it hurts? If you think it didn't hurt God to watch His Son suffer at the hands of the chief priests and soldiers, and then suffer the humiliating and painful death on the cross as He took on our sins to free us, you have an unfounded and harsh view of God the Father.

Yet **Isaiah 53:10** says:

> *"Yet it pleased the Lord to bruise Him: He hath put Him (Jesus) to grief: when thou shalt make His soul an offering for sin."*

How could it have pleased God to cause Jesus to suffer? It's because Jesus was able to abolish the penalty for sin and restore all who accepted His gift of salvation to a pre-Adam sin status. It pleased God for our sakes.

"Where, O death, is your victory? Where, O death, is your sting?" – **1 Corinthians 15:55**

The curse of spiritual death was broken, abolished by Jesus dying on the cross. God said way back in Genesis that Christ was going to conquer death, and God kept that promise by sending Jesus to the cross, a promise that was kept at painful expense to both God the Father and God the Son. But because of the outcome, it pleased God to send Jesus to the cross to suffer on our behalf.

We Can Count on God's Promises

Regrettably for some, the only promise that will be fulfilled in their lives is the promise in **2 Thessalonians 1:9,** which says, *"They* (everyone without Christ in their hearts) *will be punished in everlasting Hell, forever separated from the Lord, never to see the glory of His power."* God's glory can be seen in His love, but those who harden their hearts and reject His love while on earth will spend eternity in Hell and never see the *"glory of His power."*

Mercifully, for those who believe in Jesus, God gave a list of promises that He is incapable of breaking.

God's Promise of Love:

"This is how God showed His love among us: He sent His one and only Son into the world that we might live through Him. This is love: not that we loved God, but that He loved us and sent His Son

as an atoning sacrifice for our sins." – **1 John 4:9–10**

God's Promise of Eternal Life:

"I write these things to you who believe in the name of the Son of God so that you may know that you have eternal life." – **1 John 5:13**

God's Promise of the Holy Spirit:

"...but you know Him (Holy Spirit), for He lives with you and will be in you." – **John 14:17b**

God's Promise to Wait:

"He isn't really being slow about His (Christ's) promised return, even though it sometimes seems that way. But He is waiting, for the good reason that He is not willing that any should perish (spend eternity in Hell), and He is giving more time for sinners (you and me) to repent (accept Christ and turn from sin)." – **2 Peter 3:9**

God's Promise to Help:

"For I am the Lord your God who takes hold of your right hand and says to you, Do not fear; I will help you." – **Isaiah 41:13**

"Cast all your anxiety on Him because He cares for you." – **1 Peter 5:7**

God's Promise to Empathize with Our Weaknesses and Give Mercy and Grace:

> *"Therefore, since we have a great high priest who has ascended into heaven, Jesus the Son of God, let us hold firmly to the faith we profess. For we do not have a high priest who is unable to empathize with our weaknesses, but we have one who has been tempted in every way, just as we are—yet he (Jesus) did not sin. Let us approach God's throne of grace with confidence, so that we may receive mercy and find grace to help us in our time of need."* **– Hebrews 4:14–16**

These verses show us very clearly that Jesus, the Son of God, is very personal. He went through every temptation that we would ever go through while on earth so that He would be able to empathize with our weaknesses. How could anyone question Jesus' caring love towards us?

God's Promise of Peace:

> *"Finally, brothers and sisters, whatever is true, whatever is noble, whatever is right, whatever is pure, whatever is lovely, whatever is admirable— if anything is excellent or praiseworthy—think about such things. Whatever you have learned or received or heard from me, or seen in me—put it into practice. (If we do, we have this promise:)*

And the God of peace will be with you." –
Philippians 4:8–9

I have put this verse to the test many times, and I can attest that God has been with me and given me peace when I obey this admonition.

It is impossible to be depressed or anxious when dwelling on the good things of God. I can't lie; it takes devotion to mentally focus on the good things of God in times of trouble or doubt. Many times, I have tossed and turned night after night, trying to figure out how I was going to deal with circumstances beyond my control, only to find in the end that God already had a plan in motion behind the scenes. After His plan is accomplished, I always say to myself, *"ye of little faith."*

You would think that after forty years of walking with Christ, I would put my anxious thoughts to rest and just rely on Him. But at times, my skepticism that God cares enough to take care of me in all situations can unfortunately dictate how I mentally and physically deal with life's misfortunes. But God has always been faithful, giving me a growing foundation of being able to trust Him in all circumstances, though I am still learning that, in times of trouble, the first thing I need to do is disregard my feelings of skepticism and remember the foundation of trust that has been built up over the years of Him never disappointing me.

God's Promise of Security:

"And I give them eternal life, and they shall never perish; neither shall anyone snatch them out of

My hand. My Father, who has given them to Me, is greater than all; and no one is able to snatch them out of My Father's hand. I and My Father are one." – **John 10:28–30**

"And this is the will of Him (God) who sent me (Jesus), that I shall lose none of all those He has given to me, but raise them up at the last day." – **John 6:39**

Once you give your heart to Jesus, you will never be lost again.

God's Promise of Purpose:

"For I know the plans I have for you, declares the Lord, plans to prosper you and not to harm you, plans to give you hope and a future." – **Jeremiah 29:11**

God's Promises Will Be Fulfilled:

"Heaven and earth will disintegrate before even the smallest detail of the word of God will fail or lose its power." – **Luke 16:17**

In other words, you can count on the promises of God to be fulfilled, every last one of them—either for our benefit or for our demise.

In the past, I viewed God's fulfilment of promises in the context of how poorly I have kept promises or how poorly promises have been kept towards me. This undermined my confidence in the word *promise* as my memory of broken promises allowed the hurt associated with them to cause trust issues. After coming to Christ and receiving the gift of the Holy Spirit, I learned, through the teaching of the Spirit, that God never breaks His promises. This truth transformed my trust issues, making it possible for me to come freely to His throne of grace. Now, I come with confidence that all His promises can be accepted and claimed through the power of the Holy Spirit, which validates and executes those promises in my life.

God's Promise of Heaven:

> *"Do not let your hearts be troubled. You believe in God; believe also in me (Jesus). My Father's house has many rooms' if that were not so, would I have told you that I am going there to prepare a place for you? And if I go and prepare a place for you, I will come back and take you to be with me that you also may be where I am."* – **John 14:1–3**

What a great promise for the believer—the one I am most excited to see fulfilled.

29

HEAVEN

The final destination for the believer in Christ is Heaven. To me, Heaven is not so much about geographical placement, but what it's going to be like and what I am going to be like when I arrive. Just imagine a place without sin, death, suffering, and corruption—a place that is perfect. And we will be made perfect the instant we arrive.

Heaven must be perfect, for could you imagine living in a place for eternity that was imperfect, with imperfect people such as ourselves? As I said before, I can't wait to lay down all of my brokenness and insecurities and trade this painful body for a new, resurrected body like Christ's. After the resurrection, we will have a spiritual body suited for living in Heaven. Our new body will have no limitations; it will never know sickness or depression— it will be awesome. We will be able to eat, for Christ Himself invited us to the wedding feast of the Lamb in **Revelation 19:9:** *"Then the angel said to me* (The Apostle John), *'Write this; Blessed are those who are invited to the wedding* supper of the Lamb!' And he added, 'These are the true words of God.'" We will be able to touch and be touched, as Christ was touched by Thomas. *"Then He (Jesus) said to Thomas, 'Put your finger here, and look at My hands; and reach your hand here, and put it into my side. Do not be unbelieving, but believing.'"* (**John 20:27**). But the best thing of all is that our new resurrected body will be without sin and never decay.

We have many great things to live for on earth, but you have to admit that there are many things that make life hard for some, and just plain tragic for others. Those hardships and tragedies are not going to be known in Heaven.

I don't want to choose Heaven only because it's a better alternative than Hell. No, I want to go to Heaven because I belong there because of my relationship with Jesus Christ. My belief in Heaven should be a life-sustaining conviction. Billy Graham had that kind of conviction. He said, "My home is in Heaven. I'm just traveling through this world."[xxxix]

Hebrews 13:14 supports his conviction: *"For this world is not our home; we are looking forward to our everlasting home in Heaven."*

Some are worried that eternity in Heaven may become boring, tiresome, and through the millennia, repetitious. I look at it this way: Christ did not suffer on the cross for us to end up in a state of mediocrity. He died on the cross so His joy would be made complete—so that our joy would be made complete. I'm sure the last thing we will have to worry about is eternity becoming boring or tiresome.

It is written in **1 Corinthians 2:9,** *"That is what is meant by the Scriptures which say that no mere man has ever seen, heard, or even imagined what wonderful things God has ready for those who love the Lord Jesus. "* It seems from that verse alone that we will not be disappointed for even one day in Heaven, let alone a millennium. The fact is, our temporal mindset will be changed into an eternal mindset. We will be moved from the finite to the infinite at a moment's notice.

Yes, I look forward to that day when Heaven becomes my permanent home, when my spiritual body will become my permanent body, and as the song "Mansion Over the Hilltop" says, "we will never more wander."[xl]

30

INVITE CHRIST INTO
YOUR LIFE

In the quiet moments of life, when honest feelings of the heart speak their loudest, do you know without a shadow of a doubt, that you have peace with God?

If there is any doubt—any doubt at all—consider what is written below. Take an honest look at yourself in view of what God says in the verses below. As I've encouraged you before, please don't let pride dictate where you are going to spend eternity. Receive Jesus' offer of salvation.

The Bible says in **1 John 5:13,** *"I write these things to you who believe in the name of the Son of God so that you may know that you have eternal life."* We have a direct promise from God that we can *know* we have eternal life.

To be absolutely certain that Heaven is your final destination, you need to answer several questions honestly:

#1 – Do you see anything in yourself that would keep you out of Heaven?

Most people know they are sinful, but perhaps your answer is no. If so, **Romans 3:23** means you are wrong about that unless you have already accepted God's forgiveness for your sin: *"For all have sinned and fall short of the glory of God"*. If your answer is yes, you're in agreement with **Romans 3:23** that your relationship with God is broken because of sin.

So, what does a broken relationship with God mean? For God, it means grief that He will be separated from His creation for eternity. For us, it means the consequence of being separated from God for eternity because of our sin. **Romans 6:23a** is unequivocally clear on that point: *"For the wages of sin is death."* The word *death* in this verse means a punishment of spiritual separation of your soul from God in Hell.

#2 – How can man's problem of separation from God due to sin be rectified?

God's grief that His creation was separated from Him by sin put into action His grace towards us. God sums up His grace towards us in **Ephesians 2:8–9,** which says: *"For by grace are you saved, through faith, and this not of yourselves—it is the gift of God. Not by works, so that no one can boast."* And how did God accomplish this? By sending His Son Jesus to the cross to take the punishment we deserve, then offering that substitution of the guiltless for the guilty. **1 Peter 3:18** says. *"For Christ died for sins once for all, the righteous for the unrighteous to bring you to God,"* then offered His payment of that sin debt as a gift to us. This is the good news of **Romans 6:23b:** *"The gift of God is eternal life in Christ Jesus our Lord."*

So, though we are eternally separated from God by sin, we are offered a simple solution: receive the gift of salvation God offers by receiving Jesus Christ as our Saviour.

#3 – To receive Jesus Christ, understand and acknowledge:

- The separation between us and God can be repaired only by believing in Jesus Christ. *"I do not set aside the grace of God, for if righteousness could be gained through the law, Christ died for nothing"* **(Galatians 2:21).**

- Christ didn't stay dead. Jesus was resurrected from the grave on the third day, and now sits at the right hand of God. *"He was delivered over to death for our sins and was raised to life for our justification"* **(Romans 4:25).**

- The justification in Romans 4:25 means the action of declaring or making righteous in the sight of God. God makes us righteous in His sight by the sacrifice of Jesus on the cross, and that justification is available to any who receive Christ's gift of salvation. Upon receiving Christ, God removes the sin from the sinner's account and moves it to Jesus' account, clearing the sinner's debt. *"God made him who had no sin* (Jesus) *to be sin for us, so that in Him we might become the righteousness of God"* **(2 Corinthians 5:21).**

- We receive God's forgiveness by believing in Jesus. *"Believe in the Lord Jesus Christ and you will be saved"* (**Acts 16:31**). And **John 1:12** assures us, *"To all who received Him, to those who believed in His Name, He gave the right to become children of God."* Then, one of the greatest promises God ever made was from Jesus in **John 14:3:** *"And if I go and prepare a place for you, I will come back and take you to be with me that you may also be where I am."*

- **Receiving Christ** means having a personal relationship with Jesus, and it's a gift that must be accepted personally. No one can accept the gift of salvation for you by proxy. You are not born into the gift because of family ties, and you are not baptized into Heaven—for baptism has no redemptive qualities, no matter at what age the sacrament is completed. The purpose of baptism is to make a profession of faith to others that we have already believed in the death, burial, and resurrection of Jesus Christ, accepted His gift of salvation, and received Him into our hearts. No church affiliation is going to get you into Heaven either.

- Salvation is a free gift given to us by God on a personal level. That is why the acceptance of this gift is done personally, by believing in what Jesus Christ did on the cross by faith. The gift is very personal because if you were the only one in the whole wide world, Christ still would have gone to the cross on your behalf. Since the gift is that personal, it's only fitting that the gift must be accepted personally. That, my friends, is the demonstration of God's personal love for us in epic proportions.

- If a condemned sinners receives Jesus Christ's atoning sacrifice personally, by faith, they become justified before God. The act of justification is God's righteous act of removing the condemnation, guilt, and penalty of sin by grace. Through this act of faith, God proclaims the ungodly to be righteous, giving hope, peace, and an inheritance to the once condemned. Amen.

Receive Jesus Christ as Your Saviour

If this is the desire of your heart, and the prayer below is in agreement with what you believe—use the prayer as a guideline to ask God to forgive you.

> *Lord, I know that being judged by Your laws, I have come up short and am guilty and sinful in your sight. My sinfulness has created a separation between You and me that I cannot fix. I ask humbly for your forgiveness, by placing my faith only in what Jesus did by taking the punishment I deserved on the cross. Please allow me to accept Jesus' offer of salvation, so I can be forgiven and adopted into Your family and have Heaven's doors opened to me. Lord, I place my total trust in Jesus for my salvation. Amen.*

If you prayed that prayer, your newfound relationship with Jesus Christ means that you are now free from judgement and condemnation. You are Heaven-bound. You are a new person in Christ, thanks be to God's amazing Grace.

Now, tell someone about your decision to place your faith in Jesus Christ.

> *"For if you tell others with your own mouth that Jesus Christ is your Lord and believe in your own heart that God has raised Him from the dead, you will be saved."* – **Romans 10:9**

> *"And I assure you of this; I, (Jesus) the Messiah, will publicly honour you in the presence of God's angels if you publicly acknowledge me here on earth as your Friend."* – **Luke 12:8**

Once you trust Christ as your Saviour, your name is written in the Lamb's Book of Life. And Scripture gives us this wonderful promise from God.

> *"The one who is victorious (who received Jesus) will, like them, be dressed in white. I will never blot out the name of that person from the Book of Life, but will acknowledge that name before my Father and His angels."* – **Revelation 3:5**

Welcome into the family of God!

CONCLUSION

Thank you for reading my story in its entirety. What happened in my life shows first, how God worked in my life to bring me into a relationship with Him; second, how He never gave up on me, even when I had given up on myself; and third, how His loving grace sustained me through it all, and will continue to do so until I walk through the gates of Heaven.

It is my prayer that sharing my personal journey of both failures and victories will help you identify with some part of my story and be encouraged that God will always be there for you, no matter what you encounter in this life.

My hope is only in the resurrection of Jesus Christ. In my life, I have experienced many victories, which were brought about only by a God who heard and responded to a prayer made from the heart of a little boy so many years before. Many nights, when sleep eludes me, I lie in my bed surrounded by darkness praying to God, thanking Him for all He has given to me. I don't thank Him as much for material possessions, though I am very thankful for those, as I do for spiritual growth over the years that has produced a sense of peace, regardless of what happens. I can count on Him. He is a gift. Even though I can't protect everyone I love, I can bring them to Him in prayer and leave them there in His care. I don't know how I would cope in this life without God's grace and peace.

The world has always been a scary place; in the thirties it was a world war; and in the sixties, it was the standoff between the Soviet Union and the United States, called the Cuban Missile Crisis. More recently, we have seen the destruction of the Twin Towers in New York in the early 2000s and many other stressful situations and disasters around the world. Now there is a pandemic and, most likely, an upcoming world crisis from national debts that are becoming unmanageable. Being overly distressed by what is happening in our world today and events that are totally out of our control is only natural, so how do you find peace in the midst of this turmoil?

I find it in the promise given in **John 14:27**: *"I am leaving you with a gift—peace of mind and heart! And the peace I give isn't fragile like the peace the world gives. So don't be troubled or afraid."* God doesn't say, "Don't be concerned." He doesn't say not to do anything, and He also doesn't say troubles won't happen. But what He does say is, *"I will never leave you or forsake you"* **(Hebrews 13:5).**

I think one of the major issues today in almost anyone's life is worry, which was no different when Jesus was here on earth. That's why Jesus tells us, *"Therefore do not worry about tomorrow, for tomorrow will worry about itself. Each day has enough trouble of its own,"* **(Matthew 6:34)** and then asks, *"Can* *any one of you by worrying add a single hour to your life?"* **(Matthew 6:27).**

Basically, Jesus is saying, "Trust in Me" for He holds our lives and future: *"For He holds our lives in His hands, and He holds our feet to the path"* **(Psalm 66:9).** Jesus gives us hope where hope doesn't seem possible, peace in a world of turmoil, and a future and a home we can look forward to.

The Apostle Paul gives an outline in **Philippians 4:4–7** for the believer to possess God's peace at all times:

> *"Rejoice in the Lord always, I will say it again; Rejoice! Let your gentleness be evident to all. The Lord is near. Do not be anxious about anything, but in everything, by prayer and petition, with thanksgiving, present your requests to God. And the peace of God, which transcends all understanding will guard your hearts and your minds in Christ Jesus."*

As I've said before, God's promises cannot be broken; and the promise just read doesn't say to bring only the major things in life to Him, but everything—big or small—for He cares about every detail of our lives.

When the Apostle Paul wrote the Book of Philippians, he was in prison, waiting to be put on trial for his life—not from a comfortable office, sitting in a nice leather padded chair, sipping a hot cup of coffee. No, he wrote from a prison cell, and I can't even imagine what prison would have been like back in the first century.

So, when Paul says in **Philippians 4:6,** *"Do not be anxious about anything, but in everything, by prayer and petition, with thanksgiving, present your requests to God,"* he lived what he said; his situation gives his words a level of credibility that we can trust and put into practice in our own lives.

Do I Struggle in Life?

I struggle more than some, but maybe not as much as others. Still, my faith in Christ is rock solid. I know beyond a shadow of a doubt where I am going to end up when I die. I have that assurance because of my personal relationship with Christ. Jesus has stood with me through all the things I have encountered in this life and promises to continue to walk with me until I exuberantly walk through Heaven's gate to meet Him in person.

I can't express my gratitude enough for what Jesus Christ has done in my life. Through some exceptionally hard times that I have experienced, He's always brought comfort in ways I never thought possible. I have received strength from Him when I had no strength of my own. No darkness will ever be able to extinguish His light in my life, and when I unfortunately make the lives of others around me harder than they need to be, He shows me the changes that are needed and helps me to make those personal changes through the power of His Spirit. Changing some of my less admirable ingrained traits is very hard, but as I slowly keep working through them (I have had a few victories along the way), I become more like Him. For those who know me, I am not oblivious to the fact there's still work to be done; but like I said, the entire Christian life is a progression.

I have found, over and over again, that when I stay close to the Lord by reading His Word and praying, I am a help, not a hinderance. I become a light to others for Jesus, not a clanging, annoying cymbal. Until I get to Heaven, a battle between my new nature in Christ and my old, sinful nature will always be raging—that's a given. But I know without a shadow of doubt that accepting Christ into my life in the early eighties was the most profound and awesome decision I ever made—and one I have never regretted.

FULFILLMENT OF THE PROPHECIES

WRITTEN IN ISAIAH CHAPTER 53

I n chapter 15, titled "Prophecies," I spoke of prophecies
given in the Old Testament that were fulfilled in the New
Testament. Below is a list of verses from Isaiah 53 and their
corresponding fulfillment verses in the New Testament.

OT Prophecy	NT Fulfillment
(Isaiah 53:1) Who has believed our message, and to whom has the arm of the Lord been revealed?	(John 12:37-38) Even after Jesus had done all these miraculous signs in their presence, they still would not believe in Him. This was to fulfill the words of Isaiah the prophet: "Lord, who has believed our message and to whom has the arm of the Lord been revealed?"

OT Prophecy	NT Fulfillment
(Isaiah 53:1) Who has believed our message,	**(Romans 10:16)** But not all the Israelites accepted the good news. For Isaiah says, "Lord, who has believed our message?"
(Isaiah 53:2) He grew up before him like a tender shoot, and like a root out of dry ground. He had no beauty or majesty to attract us to him, nothing in his appearance that we should desire him.	**(Matthew 13:55-57)** Coming to his hometown, Jesus began teaching the people in their synagogue, and they were amazed. Where did this man get this wisdom and these miraculous powers? They asked, isn't this the carpenter's son? Isn't his mother's name Mary, and aren't his brothers James, Joseph, Simon, and Judas? Aren't all his sisters with us? Where then did this man get all these things? And they took offence at him. But Jesus said to them, "Only in his hometown and in his own house is a prophet without honour."
(Isaiah 53:3) He was despised and rejected by men, a man of sorrows, and familiar with suffering. Like one from whom men hide their faces he was despised, and we esteemed him not.	**(Matthew 26:67)** Then they spit in his face and struck him with their fists. Others slapped him and said, "Prophesy to us, Christ. Who hit you?" **(John 19:14-16)** It was the day of Preparation of Passover Week about the sixth hour. Here is your king, Pilate said to the Jews. But they shouted, "Take him away! Take him away! Crucify him!" "Shall I crucify your king?" Pilate asked. "We have no king but Caesar," the chief priests answered. Finally, Pilate handed him over to them to be crucified.
(Isaiah 53:4) Surely, he took up our infirmities and carried our sorrows, yet we considered him	**(Matthew 8:17)** When evening came, many who were demon-possessed were brought to him, and he drove out the spirits with a word and healed all the sick. This was to fulfill what was

OT Prophecy	NT Fulfillment
stricken by God, smitten by him and afflicted.	spoken through the prophet Isaiah: "He took up our infirmities." **(Romans 3:25)** God presented Him (Jesus) as a sacrifice of atonement through faith in his blood.
(Isaiah 53:5) But he was pierced for our transgressions, he was crushed for our iniquities; the punishment that brought us peace was upon him, and by his wounds we are healed.	**(1 Peter 2:24)** He himself bore our sins in his body on the cross, so that we might die to sins and live for righteousness; by his wounds you have been healed. **(John 19:33-34)** But when they came Jesus (on the cross) and found that he was already dead, they did not break his legs. Instead, one of the soldiers pierces Jesus' side with a spear, bringing a sudden flow of blood and water.
(Isaiah 53:6) We all, like sheep, have gone astray, each of us has turned to his own way; and the Lord has laid on him the iniquity of us all.	**(Romans 3:12)** All have turned away, they have together become worthless; **(Romans 5:8)** But God demonstrates his own love for us in this: While we were still sinners, Christ died for us.
(Isaiah 53:7) He was oppressed and afflicted, yet he did not open his mouth; he was led like a lamb to the slaughter,	**(John 1:29)** The next day John (the Baptist) saw Jesus coming towards him and said, "Look, the Lamb of God," who takes away the sin of the world!

OT Prophecy	NT Fulfillment
and as a sheep before her shearers is silent, so he did not open his mouth.	**(1 Peter 2:23)** When they hurled insults at him, he did not retaliate; when he suffered, he made no threats. Instead, he entrusted himself to him who judges justly. **(Matthew 27:12-14)** When he was accused by the chief priests and the elders, he gave no answer. Then Pilate asked him, "Don't you hear the testimony they are bringing against you?" But Jesus made no reply, not even to a single charge—to the great amazement of the governor.

THE
RELEVANCE OF
ISAIAH 53

I n the **Book of Acts,** the Lord used the prophecies of **Isaiah 53** to open the Ethiopian's eyes to salvation with the help of Philip's explanation of the verses.

Philip and the Ethiopian / Acts 8:26–35

> *"Now an angel of the Lord said to Philip, 'Go south to the road—the desert road—that goes down from Jerusalem to Gaza.' So he started out, and on his way he met an Ethiopian eunuch, an important official in charge of all the treasury of the Kandace (which means 'queen of the Ethiopians'). This man had gone to Jerusalem to worship, and on his way home was sitting in his chariot reading the Book of Isaiah the prophet. The Spirit told Philip, 'Go to that chariot and stay near it.' Then Philip ran up to the chariot and*

heard the man reading Isaiah the prophet. 'Do you understand what you are reading?' Philip asked. 'How can I,' he said, 'unless someone explains it to me?' So he invited Philip to come up and sit with him. This is the passage of Scripture the eunuch was reading: He was led like a sheep to the slaughter, and as a lamb before its shearer is silent, so he did not open his mouth. In his humiliation he was deprived of justice. Who can speak of his descendants? For his life was taken from the earth. The eunuch asked Philip, 'Tell me, please, who is the prophet talking about, himself or someone else?' Then Philip began with that very passage of Scripture and told him the good news about Jesus."

It is undeniable that Jesus Christ was the one that fulfilled, to the letter, all the prophecies written in **Isaiah 53**. God used those prophecies of Christ that the Ethiopian was reading to open his eyes to who Jesus was, by the teaching of Philip. When the Ethiopian's heart was enlightened, he immediately accepted the gift of salvation.

The Ethiopian's interaction with Philip shows us that God will bring into the lives of anyone searching for Him someone who can explain the Scripture. *"'Do you understand what you are reading?' Philip asked. 'How can I,' he said, 'unless someone explains it to me?'"* And that is the job of every believer, to be a guiding light for those who are lost and searching.

BIBLE VERSE INDEX

BIBLIOGRAPHY

Alcorn, L. (2004). *Heaven*. Carol Stream: Tyndale House Pub, Inc.

Dictionary.com. (2021). *Perish*. Retrieved from Dictionary.com: https://www.dictionary.com/browse/perish

Dwight, L. M. (n.d.). *Where One Man Reads the Bible, A Hundred Read You and Me*. Retrieved from Quotefancy.com: https://quotefancy.com/quote/797052/D-L-Moody-Where-one-man-reads-the-Bible-a-hundred-read-you-and-me

Elliott, C. (n.d.). *Just as I Am*. Retrieved from WordtoWorship.com: https://wordtoworship.com/song/8096

GotQuestions.Org. (2021, April 26). *Does Hell Exist?* Retrieved from GotQuestions.Org: https://www.gotquestions.org/does-hell-exist.html

GotQuestions.Org. (2021, April 26). *If I Do Not Forgive Others, Does That Mean My Sins Are Not Forgiven?* Retrieved from GotQuestions.Org: https://www.gotquestions.org/forgive-forgiven.html

GotQuestions.Org. (2021, April 26). *What Does It Mean When Jesus Says, "my yoke is easy and my burden is light" (Matthew 11:30)?* Retrieved from GotQuestions.Org: https://www.gotquestions.org/yoke-easy-burden-light.html

GotQuestions.Org. (2021, August 6). *What Does the Bible Say About Forgiving Yourself?* Retrieved from GotQuestions.Org: https://www.gotquestions.org/forgiving-yourself.html

GotQuestions.Org. (2021, April 26). *What Is Retribution Theology?* Retrieved from GotQuestions.Org: https://www.gotquestions.org/retribution-theology.html

GotQuestions.Org. (2021, April 26). *What Is the Conviction of Sin?* Retrieved from GotQuestions.Org: https://www.gotquestions.org/conviction-of-sin.html

GotQuestions.Org. (2021, November 15). *What Is the Definition of Grace?* Retrieved from GotQuestions.Org: https://www.gotquestions.org/definition-of-grace.html

Graham, B. (2004, June 1). *Are All Sins the Same in the Eyes of God?* Retrieved from BillyGraham.Org: https://billygraham.org/answer/are-all-sins-the-same-in-gods-eyes/

Graham, B. (2004, June 1). *What Is the Unpardonable Sin? I Am Afraid I May Have Committed It.* Retrieved from BillyGraham.Org: https://billygraham.org/answer/what-is-the-unpardonable-sin-i-am-afraid-i-may-have-committed-it/

Graham, B. (2014, May 22). *Billy Graham Quotes on Heaven.* Retrieved from BillyGraham.Org: https://billygraham.org/story/billy-graham-quotes-on-heaven/

Graham, B. (2016, March 24). *Billy Graham's Answer: What Is Sin? Are All Sins Equal in God's Eyes?* Retrieved from BillyGraham.Org: https://billygraham.org/story/billy-grahams-answer-what-is-sin-are-all-sins-equal-in-gods-eyes/

Graham, B. (2016, March 24). *Billy Graham's Answer: What Is Sin? Are All Sins Equal in God's Eyes?* Retrieved from BillyGraham.Org: https://billygraham.org/story/billy-grahams-answer-what-is-sin-are-all-sins-equal-in-gods-eyes/

Graham, B. (2020, June 21). *Why the Holy Spirit Is So Important.* Retrieved from ugchristiannews.com: https://www.ugchristiannews.com/billy-graham-why-the-holy-spirit-is-so-important/

Graham, B. (n.d.). *A Daily Process.* Retrieved from BillyGraham.Org: https://billygraham.org/devotion/a-daily-process/

Hawking, S. (2018). *Brief Answers to Big Questions.* New York: Bantam Books, Inc.

Hawking, S. (2018). *Brief Answers to the Big Questions.* New York: Bantam Books, Inc.

Hawking, S. (2018). *Brief Answers to the Big Questions.* New York: Bantam Books, Inc.

Hawking, S. (2018). *Brief Answers to the Big Quetions.* New York: Bantam Books, Inc.

Jeremiah, D. (2014). *Understanding the 66 Books of the Bible.* Goldsboro: Turning Point Ministries.

Lewis, C. S. (1946). *The Great Divorce.* San Francisco: HarperSanFrancisco.

Lewis, C. S. (1996). *Problem of Pain.* San Francisco: HarperSanFrancisco.

Lindsey, H. (1976). *The Terminal Generation.* Baker Publishing Group.

MacArthur, J. J. (2019, August 9). *Did Christ Become Sinful on Our Behalf?* Retrieved from gty.org: https://www.gty.org/library/blog/B170403/did-christ-become-sinful-on-our-behalf

Merriam-Webster.com. (2021). *Repent.* Retrieved from Merriam-Webster.com: https://www.merriam-webster.com/dictionary/repent

Ministries, D. B. (2020, May 31). *Easy Does It.* Retrieved from OBD.Org: https://odb.org/CA/2020/05/31/easy-does-it

ODB.Org. (2020, May 31). *Easy Does It.* Retrieved from ODB.Org: https://odb.org/CA/2020/05/31/easy-does-it

Roper, D. (2020, May 31). *Easy Does It.* Retrieved from ODB.Org: https://odb.org/2020/05/31

Spielberg, S. (Director). (1998). *Saving Private Ryan* [Motion Picture].

Stanphill, I. (n.d.). *Mansion Over the Hilltop.* Retrieved from WordtoWorship.com: https://wordtoworship.com/song/115788

Thoms, W. (n.d.). *William Thoms Quotes.* Retrieved from AZQuotes.com: https://www.azquotes.com/author/26247-William_Thoms

Tozer, A. W. (2007). *The Best of A. W. Tozer.* Chicago: Wingspread.

Various. (1984). *The Holy Bible.* Grand Rapids: Zondervan Publishing House.

Various. (1984). *The Holy Bible.* Grand Rapids: Zondervan Publishing.

Vitale, V. (2018, May 31). *If God Is Just, Then Why Give Eternal Punishment for Temporal Sin.* Retrieved from

Youtube.com:
https://www.youtube.com/watch?v=6sF2TTHConA&ab_ch
annel=GospeLifeBroadcastingAfrica

END NOTES

[i] Lindsey, Hal. (1976) Pg 1. *The Terminal Generation*. Grand Rapids: Baker Publishing Group.

[ii] Lewis, C.S. (1946). Pg 51. *The Great Divorce*. San Francisco: HarperSanFrancisco.

[iii] Graham, Billy. *Billy Graham's Answers: What Is Sin? Are All Sinners Equal in God's Eye?* BillGraham.Org. March 24, 2016. https://billygraham.org/story/billy-grahams-answer-what-is-sin-are-all-sins-equal-in-gods-eyes/. Accessed October 11, 2021

[iv] Vitale, Vince. *If God Is Just, Then Why Give Eternal Punishment for Temporal Sin.* Youtube.com. May 31, 2018. https://www.youtube.com/watch?v=6sF2TTHConA&ab_channel=GospeLifeBroadcastingAfrica. Accessed on October 11, 2021.

[v] GotQuestions.Org. *What Is the Definition of Grace?* GotQuestions.Org. November 15, 2021. https://www.gotquestions.org/definition-of-grace.html. Accessed on November 29,2021.

[vi] Lewis, C.S. (1996). Pg. 81. Problem of Pain. San Francisco: HarperSanFrancisco.

[vii] Lewis, C.S. (1996). Pg 81. Problem of Pain. San Francisco: HarperSanFrancisco.

[viii] GotQuestions.Org. Does Hell Exist? GotQuestions.Org. April 26, 2021. https://www.gotquestions.org/does-hell-exist.html. Accessed on October 11, 2021.

[ix] Dictionary.com. *Perish*. Dictionary.com 2021. https://www.dictionary.com/browse/perish. Accessed October 11,2021.

[x] Graham, Billy. Are All Sins the Same in the Eyes of God? BillyGraham.Org. June 1, 2004. https://billygraham.org/answer/are-all-sins-the-same-in-gods-eyes/. Accessed October 11,2021.

[xi] Merriam-Webster.com. Repent. Merriam-Webster.com. 2021. https://www.merriam-webster.com/dictionary/repent. Accessed October 11,2021.

[xii] Graham, Billy. *Billy Graham's Answers: What Is Sin? Are All Sinners Equal in God's Eye?* BillyGraham.Org. March 24, 2016. https://billygraham.org/story/billy-grahams-answer-what-is-sin-are-all-sins-equal-in-gods-eyes/. Accessed October 11, 2021

xiii Hawking, Steven. (2018). Pg. 111. Brief Answers to the Big Questions. New York: Bantam Books, Inc.

xiv Hawking, Steven. (2018). Pg. 112. Brief Answers to the Big Questions. New York: Bantam Books, Inc.

xv Hawking, Steven. (2018). Pg. 113. Brief Answers to the Big Questions. New York: Bantam Books, Inc.

xvi Hawking, Steven. (2018). Pg. 114. Brief Answers to the Big Questions. New York: Bantam Books, Inc.

xvii Jeremiah, David. (2014). Pg. 117. Understanding the 66 Books of the Bible. Goldsboro: Turning Point Ministries.

xviii MacArthur, John and Jeremiah Johnson. *Did Christ Become Sinful on Our Behalf?* Gty.org. August, 9, 2019. https://www.gty.org/library/blog/B170403/did-christ-become-sinful-on-our-behalf. Accessed October 11, 2021.

xix Alcorn, Larry. (2004). Pg 140. *Heaven.* Carol Stream: Tyndale House Pub, Inc.

xx GotQuestions.Org. What is the Conviction of Sin? GoQuestions.Org. April 26, 2021. https://www.gotquestions.org/conviction-of-sin.html. Accessed October 11, 2021.

xxi Graham, Billy. *Why the Holy Spirit Is So Important.* Ugchristiannews.com. June 21, 2020. https://www.ugchristiannews.com/billy-graham-why-the-holy-spirit-is-so-important/. Accessed October 11, 2021.

xxii Graham, Billy. What is the unpardonable sin? I am afraid I may have committed it. BillyGraham.Org. June 1, 2004. https://billygraham.org/answer/what-is-the-unpardonable-sin-i-am-afraid-i-may-have-committed-it/. Accessed October 11, 2021.

xxiii Vitale, Vince. *If God Is Just, Then Why Give Eternal Punishment for Temporal Sin.* Youtube.com. May 31, 2018. https://www.youtube.com/watch?v=6sF2TTHConA&ab_channel=GospeLifeBroadcastingAfrica. Accessed on October 11, 2021.

xxiv GotQuestions.Org. *What Does the Bible Say About Forgiving Yourself?* GotQuestions.Org. August 6, 2021. https://www.gotquestions.org/forgiving-yourself.html. Accessed October 11, 2021.

xxv GotQuestions.Org. *If I Do Not Forgive Others, Does That Mean My Sins Are Not Forgiven?* GotQuestions.Org. August 26, 2021. https://www.gotquestions.org/forgive-forgiven.html. Accessed October 11, 2021.

xxvi GotQuestions.Org. What does it mean when Jesus says, "my yoke is easy and my burden is light" (Matthew 11:30)? GotQuestions.Org. April 26, 2021. https://www.gotquestions.org/yoke-easy-burden-light.html. Accessed October 11, 2021.

xxvii Graham, Billy. *A Daily Process.* BillyGraham.Org. October 2. https://billygraham.org/devotion/a-daily-process/. Accessed on October 11, 2021.

xxviii Vitale, Vince. *If God Is Just, Then Why Give Eternal Punishment for Temporal Sin.* Youtube.com. May 31, 2018. https://www.youtube.com/watch?v=6sF2TTHConA&ab_channel=GospeLifeBroadcastingAfrica. Accessed on October 11, 2021.

xxix Tozer, A.W. (2007) Pg 185. *The Best of A. W. Tozer.* Chicago: Wingspread.

xxx Roper, David. H. *Easy Does It.* ODB.Org. May 31, 2020. https://odb.org/2020/05/31. Accessed October 11, 2021.

xxxi Roper, David. H. *Easy Does It.* ODB.Org. May 31, 2020. https://odb.org/2020/05/31. Accessed October 11, 2021.

xxxii Vitale, Vince. *If God Is Just, Then Why Give Eternal Punishment for Temporal Sin.* Youtube.com. May 31, 2018. https://www.youtube.com/watch?v=6sF2TTHConA&ab_channel=GospeLifeBroadcastingAfrica. Accessed on October 11, 2021.

xxxiii Elliott, Charlotte. *Just As I Am.* WordtoWorship.Com (N.D). https://wordtoworship.com/song/8096. Accessed October 11, 2021.

xxxiv Elliott, Charlotte. *Just As I Am.* WordtoWorship.Com (N.D). https://wordtoworship.com/song/8096. Accessed October 11, 2021.

xxxv GotQuestions.Org. What Is Retribution Theology? GotQuestions.Org. April 26, 2021. https://www.gotquestions.org/retribution-theology.html. Accessed October 11, 2021.

xxxvi Moody, Dwight, L. When One Man Reads the Bible, A Hundred Read You and Me. Quotefancy.com. (N.D.). https://quotefancy.com/quote/797052/D-L-Moody-Where-one-man-reads-the-Bible-a-hundred-read-you-and-me. Accessed October 11,2021.

[xxxvii] Thoms, Williams. *William Thoms Quotes*. AzQuotes.com. (N.D.). https://www.azquotes.com/author/26247-William_Thoms. Accessed October 10, 2021.

[xxxviii] Spielberg, Steven. *Saving Private Ryan*. Dreamworks Pictures. July 24, 1998.

[xxxix] Graham, Billy. *Billy Graham Quotes on Heaven*. BillyGraham.Org. May 22, 2014. https://billygraham.org/story/billy-graham-quotes-on-heaven/. Accessed October 11, 2021.

[xl] Stanphill, Ira. *Mansion Over the Hilltop*. WordtoWorship.com. (N.D.). https://wordtoworship.com/song/115788. Accessed October 11, 2021.